The Border Guide

CMAS Border & Migration Studies Series

THE BORDER GUIDE
Institutions and Organizations of
the United States – Mexico Borderlands

Milton H. Jamail
Margo Gutiérrez

Revised & updated edition of
*The United States–Mexico
Border: A Guide to Institutions,
Organizations, and Scholars*

 CMAS Books
Center for Mexican American Studies
University of Texas at Austin • 1992

A CENTER FOR MEXICAN AMERICAN STUDIES BOOK

Editor: Víctor J. Guerra
Assistant Editor: Martha Vogel
Book Design: Jace Graf, V. J. Guerra

Publication of this book was assisted by a grant from the Inter-University Program for Latino Research.

Library of Congress Cataloging-in-Publication Data

Jamail, Milton H.
    The border guide : institutions and organizations of the United States–Mexico borderlands / by Milton H. Jamail and Margo Gutiérrez.
—2nd ed., updated and rev.
        p. cm.
    Rev. ed. of: The United States–Mexico border, a guide to institutions, organizations, and scholars. 1980.
    Includes bibliographical references.
    ISBN 0–292–70778–9 — ISBN 0–292–70779–7 (pbk.)
    1. Mexican-American Border Region—Societies, etc.—Directories.
I. Gutiérrez, Margo.   II. Jamail, Milton H. United States–Mexico border, a guide to institutions, organizations, and scholars.
III. Title.
F787.J35 1990
303.48'273072—dc20   90–35124

First Edition, 1992. Manufactured in the United States of America.

CONTENTS

PREFACE

This volume is a completely updated and revised edition of *The United States–Mexico Border: A Guide to Institutions, Organizations, and Scholars*, published in 1980 by the Latin American Area Center of the University of Arizona. Although the general structure for the guide remains much the same as in the 1980 edition, we have reorganized much of the data and added several new sections. These include a select bibliography on borderlands topics compiled by Margo Gutiérrez, and a brief guide to conducting library research on borderlands topics. A list of border chambers of commerce also has been added, and the section on local federal officials has been reorganized. In addition, the format has been redesigned to make the guide more accessible.

We have been gathering new information for this edition since 1980. Between 1988 and 1990, one of the compilers visited each of the principal border cities to update information. We have made every reasonable effort to be as current as possible. As with any data of this kind, however, some details will date even before we go to press. This is unavoidable; where practical, though, we have described how we obtained the information, so that readers may update it themselves when necessary.

We also made the effort to be as accurate and inclusive as possible. Undoubtedly, some errors and unintentional exclusions have been made. This is inevitable, however, when dealing with a geographical area so large and a subject so broad. Due to limitations of space, furthermore, some categories of groups have been excluded intentionally. For instance, the guide does not include social or social service groups such as Rotary, Kiwanis, or Lions clubs, nor does it include community action groups. Business associations by and large have also been excluded. Listings of these and other local groups can usually be obtained from local chambers of commerce or telephone directories.

In the twelve years since the first edition, scholarship concerning the region has mushroomed. We have not, however, listed individual scholars in this edition because the Center for U.S.–Mexican Studies at the University of California, San Diego, and the Colegio de la Frontera Norte in Tijuana copublish the *International Guide to Research on Mexico*, a biennial directory of individuals conducting research on U.S.–Mexican issues, including the borderlands. We direct our readers to this excellent reference work.

Due to the abundance of information available on the United States and the relative ease with which it can be found, the guide is more complete concerning the U.S. side of the border. Wherever possible, information on the Mexican side is included, even if fragmentary.

This guide is an attempt to compose an orderly schema out of a myriad of institutions and organizations that at first sight present a rather chaotic picture. It's a risky enterprise. As one longtime border resident succinctly phrased it: "Everything seems to work very well along the border until somebody attempts to organize it." We certainly hope this work will prove to be an exception.

Although it is not possible to thank all of the people who have helped to make this guide possible, we would like to recognize the contributions of Marta S. Ayala, Augie Bareño, Anne Callaghan, Jorge Carrillo, Paul Ganster, Guillermo García, Larry Herzog, Adriana Mendiolea, Steve Mumme, Elisa Sánchez, Roberto Sánchez, Iliana Sonntag, Paul Storing, and Jesús Velasco. Special thanks to Rodolfo de la Garza and Laura Gutiérrez-Witt for their constant support and encouragement, and to Víctor Guerra and Martha Vogel for their editorial guidance. Finally, we dedicate this book to the memory of Cristóbal Aldrete, who freely and cheerfully shared his expertise, and always with a sense of humor.

The Border Guide

U.S.–Mexico Border Region

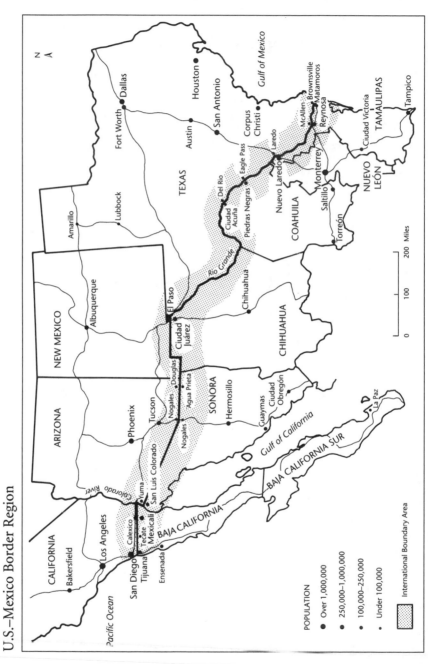

Reprinted, by permission, from Lawrence A. Herzog, *Where North Meets South: Cities, Space, and Politics on the U.S.–Mexico Border* (Austin: Center for Mexican American Studies, University of Texas at Austin, 1990), 34.

1 INTRODUCTION: THE UNITED STATES–MEXICO BORDER

For purposes of this book, the U.S.–Mexico borderlands will be defined roughly as a hundred-mile-wide strip of land centered on the international boundary line, which stretches from the Gulf of Mexico to the Pacific Ocean. To one side of the nearly 2,000-mile-long border lies the United States, one of the most highly industrialized, technologically advanced countries in the world. To the other side lies Mexico, a developing country. At this economic level, it is important to note that Mexico's leading sources of revenue—petroleum, *maquiladoras,* tourism, and remittances sent home from migrant workers—are all tied to, and in many ways dependent on, the United States. It is unlikely that there are two more distinctly different countries anywhere sharing a border; the political and social systems of the two countries are also radically different. Failure to take the differences into account often leads to misunderstanding between citizens of the two countries.

The international boundary line between the United States and Mexico was established in the mid-nineteenth century; it was then that the seeds of many contemporary border issues and problems were sown. Where before it had been just a river along which towns had naturally settled, the Rio Grande now became a dividing line. And most towns along the nonriver portion of the U.S.–Mexico border owe their location to the boundary itself.

In recent years, the U.S.–Mexico border region has been experiencing a rapid increase in population. At the turn of the century only 70,000 people lived along the border. In 1990 it was estimated that almost ten million people lived in the borderlands, with two of Mexico's six largest cities located there. Along the Mexican side of the border the population surge is caused by high unemployment in the Mexican interior, coupled with both higher wage scales along the border and the area's proximity to the United States. On the U.S. side, lack of a strong trade union movement and relatively low wage scales have attracted new businesses to the area; this, plus a general shift in population to the Sunbelt region, account for the growth.

Mexico's northern border region is generally more prosperous than other sections of the country. In contrast, some of the most economically depressed areas of the United States are located in the borderlands. Even here, however, per capita income is at least three times higher than in Mexico. Since 1980, with the decline of the petroleum-related prosperity enjoyed by Mexico and Texas in the prior decade, the region has been in the throes of an economic crisis. The value of the peso has dropped sharply: in 1980 the peso was pegged at 25 pesos to 1 U.S. dollar; in mid-1992 the value is 3,300 to 1. This "crash" and the resulting inflation have been particularly hard on the Mexican population. On the Texas side, the recession in the state's economy has been accompanied by a rise in unemployment in the border counties of Starr, Hidalgo, and Cameron, already among the poorest counties in the country. And the fall of the peso has drastically hurt merchants along the entire length of the border.

Whereas in 1975 Mexican petroleum and Mexico's newfound wealth were the main topics of conversation in the borderlands, today the words heard most often are *maquiladoras,* free trade, and drugs. The *maquiladora,* or in-bond manufacturing, program allows foreign companies to set up plants in Mexico to which they can ship raw materials and components duty-free for assembly or further processing and subsequent exportation. These assembly plants, called *maquiladoras,* traditionally have produced principally electronic components, automotive parts, or clothing, but are expanding into other areas. The number of *maquiladoras* has increased greatly during the 1980s, and they are perceived by some economic development analysts as the "salvation" of the border economy. In May 1991, the U.S. Congress gave President Bush "fast-track" authority to negotiate a free-trade agreement with Mexico. When this agreement is finally negotiated, it will have a profound impact on U.S.–Mexico relations at the border. Contraband trafficking in illegal drugs in the borderlands also appears to have risen sharply in the past decade. But by far the largest growth industry along the border has been the *casa de cambio,* the money exchange shop. Signs displaying the daily rate of exchange can be found on almost any block in the immediate vicinity of every Mexican border crossing in the United States.

The border regions of the United States and Mexico have long suffered from neglect, however benign. But the 1970s saw the neglect transformed into fascination. In the 1980s this increasing interest in the borderlands started to become institutionalized. The private sector, for instance, generated the Border Trade Alliance, which in a short period has become one of the most important organizations dealing with *maquiladora* and border trade concerns.

The trend is nowhere more evident than in academia. The Colegio de la Frontera Norte (COLEF) in Tijuana, an institution focusing exclusively on border issues, opened in 1982; San Diego State University set up the Institute for Regional Studies of the Californias in 1983; and the University of New Mexico established its International Transboundary Resources Center in 1986. The University of California, San Diego, began its Center for U.S.–Mexican Studies in 1980, and though its focus is on more general relations between the two countries, it does take an active interest in border topics. New periodicals concentrating on border affairs include the *Journal of Borderlands Studies, Twin Plant News, Cultura Norte*, and *Frontera Norte*. There is even a Japanese publication, *Third Coast*, that looks exclusively at U.S.–Mexican border issues.

New borderland institutions have also emerged in the public sector. In 1986, for example, the city of San Diego opened its Office of Binational Affairs, and in 1987 the county of San Diego established its Department of Transborder Affairs. The creation of these departments signals a recognition of the increased interdependence between the cities of San Diego and Tijuana. (Of course, interdependence has long been recognized in some quarters: the International Boundary and Water Commission, the only binational agency concerned with border affairs, in 1989 completed one hundred years of operation.) Although some border-related agencies have ceased to exist during the past decade—including the Organization of Border Cities and Counties and the Southwest Border Regional Commission in the United States, and Mexico's "Coordinating Commission of the Program for Development of Border Areas and Free Zones"—in the 1990s we can certainly expect to see new governmental organizations focusing on borderland issues.

Today, the most important borderland issues involve the flow of people and goods between the two countries. This includes the everyday crossings of both documented and undocumented Mexicans who work in the United States, tourists and shoppers from both countries, the export-import businesses, and the illegal drug trade. Other subjects likely to become even more important in the near future are water supply, pollution of shared waterways, and sewage disposal. Topics of local and regional importance will be discussed in Chapter 2.

Residents sometimes question whether governmental involvement and scholarly investigation can help resolve any of the border's urgent problems. The border certainly presents countless opportunities for disagreement. The vast majority of interchanges between the United States and

Mexico take place on the border. There are over 185 million legal crossings into the United States from Mexico each year. And the border area holds at least eight million people, sharing communities divided by an artificial, political boundary line. It is no wonder that there are conflicts.

What is remarkable, however, is the degree of cross-boundary cooperation that exists. U.S. and Mexican border communities are highly interdependent, and all along the frontier informal mechanisms have been established for avoiding or resolving conflict in everyday affairs. Many problems are handled in this extralegal fashion, in order to bypass the cumbersome and time-consuming processes involving the bureaucracies in Washington, D.C., and Mexico City—bureaucracies that are often perceived as unaware of, or unresponsive to, the needs of their constituents. Few people in the United States or Mexico living away from the border appreciate the complex interrelationships that exist between communities divided by the border. In fact, residents of the border region often feel misunderstood by the outside world.

By making a wide range of information available in one volume, the *Border Guide* seeks to promote productive dialogue across the border, and to contribute to the efforts of people on both sides of the border to better understand and negotiate the borderlands.

2 BORDER COMMUNITIES: DESCRIPTIONS & LOCAL LISTINGS

2.1 LOWER RIO GRANDE VALLEY–TAMAULIPAS BORDER REGION

More than one million people live in the southernmost region of Texas and the northeastern area of Mexico, inhabiting a one-hundred-mile strip of land along the Rio Grande, or Río Bravo, as it is known in Mexico. On the U.S. side the area is known as the "Magic Valley," due to its long growing season for fruits and vegetables, and its mild winters that are attractive to tourists. It is also described as the "Valley of Tears," however; this sobriquet refers to the acute poverty in which many of its residents live. The Valley counties of Cameron, Hidalgo, and Starr are among the poorest in the United States. One of the most dramatic aspects of this poverty are the much-discussed *colonias:* unincorporated vil lages in the Valley that lack adequate water supply and sewage disposal facilities. The Tamaulipan side is characterized by incomes above Mexico's national average. Yet these incomes are less than one-third of those in the adjacent Texas counties. It is this contrast, in part, that leads many workers to cross over to work in the United States.

In the Valley, the main crossing points between the United States and Mexico are the bridge at Reynosa–Hidalgo, the bridge at Progreso–Nuevo Progreso, and two bridges at Brownsville–Matamoros. The Reynosa–Hidalgo bridge was recently expanded. A new bridge is under construction at Los Indios, near Harlingen, and an additional bridge at Brownsville–Matamoros is under discussion.

The Valley's main industries are tourism (including more than 125,000 annual "winter visitors," who spent $161 million in 1987), agriculture (particularly citrus, although the 1983 freeze put many of the smaller citrus farms out of business), retail trade with Mexico, export-import business with Mexico, and shrimping. In December 1988, Fruit of the Loom announced the construction of a textile mill in Harlingen that will employ 800 people upon opening, with an additional 2,400 workers scheduled to be employed within ten years. The company plans to build a plant in Matamoros.

One of the most crucial issues facing the Valley is its water supply. Agriculture has traditionally claimed most of the water from the Rio Grande. Dams constructed at the turn of the century, and expanded and improved in recent years, provide flood control and water supply.

Without these dams, the great boom in agriculture and the subsequent population growth would not have been possible. Today, however, agriculture must compete with municipal and industrial users for a very limited supply of water—and this competition exists on both sides of the border.

The Valley has several population groups that are difficult to enumerate. In addition to its winter visitors, the area is home to approximately 100,000 migrant farm workers between October and April. An unknown number of undocumented workers also live in or pass through the Valley. Whereas in the past this group was composed primarily of Mexicans, it has recently included many Central Americans.

Central American immigrants have been entering the United States through the Rio Grande Valley since the late 1970s. Mostly undocumented, they cross here because it provides the nearest land border to their home countries of Guatemala, El Salvador, Nicaragua, and Honduras. Some of these immigrants have fled political violence; others are seeking increased economic opportunities (that are so limited in Central America partially because of the political conflicts there). Most do not want to stay in the Valley, but prefer to make their way quickly to communities in Houston, New Orleans, Miami, New York, Washington, Los Angeles, and San Francisco. Many are detained by U.S. immigration officials. The result has been that the area has become a bottleneck. The Valley is easy to enter from Mexico, but difficult to leave because of immigration checkpoints on all roads leading north. This has placed an additional burden on the already strained infrastructure of the Valley's private and public sectors. Although it has contributed to an increased awareness in the Valley of events in Central America, it has also led to misunderstandings between local residents—the majority of whom are themselves Hispanic—and the recently arrived Central Americans.

Brownsville, Texas–Matamoros, Tamaulipas

The Brownsville–Matamoros metropolitan area is the southernmost crossing point between the United States and Mexico. Located 275 miles southeast of San Antonio and 150 miles northeast of Monterrey, the area is increasing in population at a rapid rate. Brownsville has a population of just over 100,000, 81 percent of whom are Mexican American, and the *municipio* of Matamoros has a population of 300,000. The two cities are contiguous, with only the river separating them.

The Brownsville economy is based upon commerce with Mexico, retail sales to Mexican shoppers, tourism, light industry, shrimping, and revenue from the Port of Brownsville. The port not only serves the Texas Rio Grande Valley, but also Matamoros, Reynosa, Nuevo Laredo, and Monterrey. Due especially to the general recession in the Mexican economy and the drop in oil prices, the Port of Brownsville is not as prosperous as it was in the 1970s.

Matamoros is an agricultural supply center for the surrounding region, a center for *maquiladoras,* and a tourist attraction for Texas' winter visitors.

Some of the area's institutions of higher education are a technical institute and a branch of the Colegio de la Frontera Norte (COLEF) in Matamoros, and the two-year Texas Southmost College and the University of Texas at Brownsville (formerly Pan American University, recently incorporated into the University of Texas system).

Major topics of discussion between Brownsville and Matamoros include the construction of a new bridge and improved communication between the two cities.

McAllen, Texas–Reynosa, Tamaulipas

Located about sixty miles north of the Brownsville–Matamoros area, the McAllen–Reynosa region is another major crossing point on the border. Reynosa is separated from McAllen by seven miles.

The McAllen–Edinburg–Mission (Hidalgo County) Metropolitan Statistical Area (MSA) has a population of 384,000, of which 83 percent is Mexican American. It is one of the poorest MSAs in the United States, and in early 1989 had an unemployment rate of 16 percent. Ironically, in late 1988 the magazine *Psychology Today* rated the McAllen–Edinburg–Mission area as one of the least stressful areas to live in in the United States.

The center of the region on the U.S. side is McAllen, founded in 1902. A city of 75,000, McAllen has an economy that depends on retail sales to Mexican shoppers, agricultural interests, the apparel industry, the oil and natural gas industries, and tourism.

Reynosa (pop. 300,000) was established in 1749 at a site about fifteen miles upriver from its present location, where it moved in 1802. A large Petróleos Mexicanos (PEMEX) petrochemical complex is located in Reynosa, as are several *maquiladoras.* The city serves as a supply center for the agricultural interests on the Mexican side of the Valley, and as a tourist center.

Educational institutions include a technical school and a branch of Colegio de la Frontera Norte (COLEF) in Reynosa, and the University of Texas–Pan American in Edinburg (formerly Pan American University, recently incorporated into the University of Texas system).

Starr and Zapata Counties, Texas–Gustavo Díaz Ordaz, Camargo, Miguel Alemán, and Ciudad Mier, Tamaulipas

Midway between Brownsville–Matamoros and the two Laredos are Starr County, Texas (pop. 40,500), and the adjacent area of Tamaulipas, Mexico. On the U.S. side of the border, Roma and Rio Grande City are the most important cities. The population centers on the Mexican side are Gustavo Díaz Ordaz (pop. 18,000), Camargo (pop. 16,000), Miguel Alemán (pop. 19,600), and Ciudad Mier (pop. 3,100). Camargo and Ciudad Mier are among the oldest settlements on the border. Starr County relies upon trade with Mexico, agriculture, and ranching, and has also become an infamous site for drug trafficking.

The construction of Falcon Dam in 1954 helped to alleviate the region's periodic flooding. The resulting Falcon Lake submerged the communities of Zapata, Texas, and Guerrero, Tamaulipas, however, completely transforming this area of the borderlands. (These two towns were essentially rebuilt in new locations.)

Zapata County (pop. 9,300) is located just north of Starr County (and largely outside of the Lower Rio Grande Valley proper). Its economy depends upon tourism generated by fishing on Falcon Lake.

2.2 LAREDO–NUEVO LAREDO (LOS DOS LAREDOS)

The contiguous cities of Laredo, Texas, and Nuevo Laredo, Tamaulipas, form one of the most important crossing points on the border for commerce. They are situated 150 miles southwest of San Antonio and 150 miles north of Monterrey, on the highway connecting the main industrial centers of both countries.

Founded in 1755, Laredo is one of the oldest settlements on the border. The city not only belonged at one time or another to Spain, France, Mexico, the Confederacy, the Republic of Texas, and the United States, but was also the capital of the Republic of the Rio Grande in the late 1830s and early 1840s. The original settlement was on the north bank, and after Texas was annexed by the United States and the Rio Grande became the international dividing line, some residents moved across the river and established Nuevo Laredo in the 1840s. Nowhere along the border are two cities more interdependent, or cross-border familial ties more extensive. Relations between the two communities are generally congenial; an example of these good relations is Los Tecolotes de los Dos Laredos (a Nuevo Laredo franchise of the Mexican professional baseball league), which plays one-third of its home games in Laredo.

Laredo is the seat of Webb County. It has a population estimated to be 120,000, 94 percent of which is Mexican American. Nuevo Laredo's population exceeds 300,000. The economy of the two Laredos (or "Los Dos Laredos," as they are commonly known) revolves around the export-import trade, tourism in Nuevo Laredo, and retail sales in Laredo. Laredo has the highest per capita retail sales rate in the United States, primarily due to sales to Mexican shoppers. Tourism is important to the economy of Laredo as well, and both Nuevo Laredo and Laredo serve as supply centers for farming and ranching communities. The oil and gas industry, once a vital part of the Laredo economy, has experienced a marked decline in recent years. The number of *maquiladoras* in Nuevo Laredo has increased, but Nuevo Laredo still lags behind the five major centers (Tijuana, Mexicali, Nogales, Ciudad Juárez, and Matamoros).

Another, less-discussed facet of the area's economy is contraband, including the smuggling of drugs into the United States, and the illegal exportation of arms to Mexico. Until recently, the smuggling into Mexico of electrical appliances and electronic merchandise purchased in Laredo was widespread, but that activity has diminished due to changes in Mexico's tariff structure.

Institutions of higher learning include a branch of the Colegio de la Frontera Norte (COLEF) and a technical school in Nuevo Laredo, and Laredo Junior College and Laredo State University in Laredo, Texas. The latter was incorporated into the Texas A&M University system in 1989.

The most important issues under discussion in this area involve questions of trade, bridge building, and the water quality of the Rio Grande. Obviously, peso devaluations have significantly affected trade between the communities.

The area's third bridge, located north of the two Laredos at Dolores–Colombia, became operational in 1991. On the Texas side, the new bridge is situated on the former Dolores Ranch; the bridge site and the road connecting it to the city have been annexed by Laredo. The Mexican town of Colombia is situated in the small section of the state of Nuevo León that touches the border. The new bridge and improved and expanded highway connections to the state capital of Monterrey are expected to absorb a great deal of the truck traffic coming out of Monterrey through the two Laredos.

Water quality is a crucial issue affecting the two cities. While Laredo, Texas, must meet U.S. standards for sewage treatment, Nuevo Laredo discharges untreated sewage directly into the river. Discussions of this problem have been held between the United States and Mexico for a number of years; in 1989, a binational agreement was signed that provides for the construction of a sewage disposal plant in Nuevo Laredo.

2.3 EAGLE PASS–PIEDRAS NEGRAS— DEL RIO–ACUÑA REGION

Eagle Pass, Texas–Piedras Negras, Coahuila

These two communities are located 140 miles southwest of San Antonio and about 100 miles north of Laredo. With the international bridge linking their central business districts, they have long enjoyed a close relationship.

Eagle Pass (pop. 25,000) is the seat of Maverick County. Over 90 percent of its residents are Mexican American; approximately 25 percent are migrant laborers who leave each spring to harvest crops in other regions of the United States. Although farming, ranching, and tourism (especially during the deer-hunting season in the fall) help to bolster the local economy, the community depends primarily upon commerce with Mexico. In the early 1980s, before the devaluation of the Mexican peso, it was estimated that 70 percent of Eagle Pass' retail sales were to residents of northern Mexico. Shoppers from Mexico contribute to both the private and public sector (via sales taxes), but they place additional strains on the city's public services.

Piedras Negras has a population of over 100,000. The railroad, the government, the service and tourist industries, and *maquiladoras* are the main sources of employment. Just to the west of the city, coal mines and a coal-fired electricity-generating plant provide additional employment opportunities.

Del Rio, Texas–Ciudad Acuña, Coahuila

Unlike most other Texas border cities, whose downtown areas directly face their Mexican neighbors, Del Rio faces away from Ciudad Acuña. Several miles separate downtown Del Rio from the international bridge, giving the city an ambience different from that of most other U.S. border cities. Its distance from the border limits the amount of cross-border pedestrian traffic. Another of Del Rio's distinctive features is that its population is roughly equivalent in size to that of Ciudad Acuña: Del Rio contains almost 35,000 residents (of whom approximately 70 percent are Mexican American), and Ciudad Acuña is home to more than 50,000 people. In most other pairs of border cities, the Mexican city is considerably larger than its U.S. counterpart.

Del Rio is the seat of Val Verde County, which is Texas' principal sheep-raising and wool-producing area. The largest single employer in the county, however, is Laughlin Air Force Base. County residents breathed a collective sigh of relief when the base was excluded from the December 1988 list of military installations slated for cutback or closure. Because neither sheep farming nor base operations are border related, Del Rio is considerably less dependent upon its Mexican counterpart then most other U.S. border communities. There is, of course, a certain amount of trade with Mexico, as well as retail sales to Mexican shoppers. Additional economic activities include light manufacturing, tourism, and agricultural supplies.

Until the late 1960s, poor highway and rail connections isolated Ciudad Acuña from the interior of Mexico. For example, Acuña residents going to the nearby Mexican city of Piedras Negras found it easier to get there by traveling on the U.S. side. The city's isolation earned it the title of "the independent republic of Acuña." Today the city is a supply center for the large sheep-raising and wool-producing region around Acuña. Tourism, retail sales to residents of Del Rio, and the few *maquiladoras* also account for much of the city's revenue.

The construction of Amistad Dam about fifteen miles upriver, which took place in the late 1960s, has brought increased revenue from tourism to both cities.

One of the most pressing issues confronting the two cities was relieved by the construction of a new international bridge in 1987. The old bridge was so narrow that it was barely possible for two cars to cross at the same time.

2.4 BIG BEND–COAHUILAN AND CHIHUAHUAN DESERTS REGION

This sparsely populated region of the border extends from the area just west of Del Rio–Ciudad Acuña to the area just below El Paso–Ciudad Juárez. Its only binational population center is Presidio, Texas–Ojinaga, Chihuahua. The unincorporated city of Presidio has 3,000 residents; Ojinaga is much larger, with an estimated population of approximately 50,000. Presidio's economy revolves around agriculture, and around the border itself. Presidio has no city government—most government services affecting it are located sixty miles away in Marfa, the seat of Presidio County. Ojinaga is the terminus for the Chihuahua-Pacific Railroad, a collection point for the *candelilla* wax industry, and the site of some light industry.

The Big Bend area is extremely large, yet has few legal border crossings. Apart from the international bridge at Presidio–Ojinaga, they include a crossing by boat or horseback from the Big Bend National Park to Boquillas, Coahuila, and a private bridge located just northeast of the park at the entrance to the La Linda mine in Mexico. Due to the remote nature of the region, there is a great deal of contraband traffic in both directions.

Border Focus Group

CHIHUAHUAN DESERT RESEARCH INSTITUTE (CDRI)

This institute, which is concerned with the natural history of the Chihuahuan Desert region of the United States and Mexico, conducts field trips and seminars on related topics. Schedules, newsletters, and membership information may be obtained by writing the CDRI.

Chihuahuan Desert Research Institute
P.O. Box 1334
Alpine, Texas 79831-1334
(915) 837-8370
Executive Director: Dennis J. Miller

2.5   EL PASO–CIUDAD JUAREZ

El Paso del Norte has been an important crossing point on the Rio Grande since the sixteenth century. Today the El Paso–Ciudad Juárez area, lying 1,200 river miles from the Gulf of Mexico and more than 700 land miles from the Pacific Ocean, is located where the river border gives way to a land border. The downtown areas of the two cities face each other, separated only by the Rio Grande.

The city of El Paso (pop. 517,000) has an economy closely tied to Mexico; retail sales to Mexican shoppers is one of its mainstays. Military installations, the railroad, and the apparel industry are also very important. El Paso vies with San Diego County for the largest number of crossings into the United States, and with Laredo for the largest volume of commercial traffic.

Ciudad Juárez has a population estimated to be close to one million. Tourism, trade with the United States, the lumber industry, and agriculture are important sectors of the city's economy. But at the heart of the Ciudad Juárez economy are the many *maquiladoras*, which employ over 113,000 people.

El Paso and Ciudad Juárez are highly interdependent. Aside from the cities' formal bureaucratic interactions, informal yet regularized communication takes place between academics, government officials, and members of the private sectors of the two communities.

Educational institutions on the Mexican side include the Universidad Autónoma de Ciudad Juárez, the Escuela Superior de Agricultura Hermanos Escobar, a regional technical institute, a medical school, and a branch of the Colegio de la Frontera Norte. The University of Texas at El Paso, El Paso Community College, and a branch of Texas Tech Medical School are located in El Paso.

The issues of most concern for El Paso and Ciudad Juárez include maintaining an open flow of commerce and people, regulating air quality, and conserving the scarce water resources shared by the two communities. In late 1990, a new eight-lane bridge was opened at Zaragosa, approximately twenty miles south of downtown El Paso.

2.6 NEW MEXICO–CHIHUAHUA BORDERLANDS

The state of New Mexico shares an extensive border with Mexico, yet there are few official border crossings, and little economic activity in the region. Although the counties of Doña Ana, Luna, and Hidalgo adjoin the border, their county seats (Las Cruces, Deming, and Lordsburg, respectively) are located in the interior.

The most important crossing on the New Mexico border is the village of Columbus. Best known as the site of a 1916 raid by Francisco ("Pancho") Villa, Columbus has a population of 500. Although its official limits include the border, the village itself is situated two and one-half miles to the north. Across the border from Columbus lies the city of General Rodrigo Quevedo (pop. 5,000).

The economy of the Columbus–General Quevedo area depends upon ranching; the importation of cattle into the United States is the major economic activity at the Columbus–General Quevedo border crossing. Issues under discussion by the two communities include curtailing contraband, improving border-crossing procedures, creating an industrial park to attract *maquiladoras,* and building rail spurs to connect the Columbus–General Quevedo area to the main rail networks of each country.

Antelope Wells lies approximately ninety miles southwest of Columbus in a remote, sparsely populated region. Although it is a legal crossing, it mainly serves as a port of entry for Mexican cattle being imported into the United States.

The establishment of a new crossing into New Mexico that would give the state direct access to Ciudad Juárez had been under consideration for years. Recently, a new site was officially designated at Santa Teresa, just west of El Paso, and will likely open by fall 1992.

New Mexico State University, a center of much border-related research, is located in Las Cruces.

2.7   ARIZONA–SONORA BORDERLANDS

The Arizona–Sonora borderlands traverse four counties on the U.S. side (Cochise [Bisbee, county seat], Santa Cruz [Nogales], Pima [Tucson], and Yuma [Yuma]), and nine *municipios* on the Mexican side (Agua Prieta, Naco, Cananea, Santa Cruz, Nogales, San Luis Río Colorado, Caborca, Saric, and Puerto Peñasco). The Cochise County–Cananea area, the Nogales area, and the Yuma–San Luis Río Colorado area will be discussed below. Pima County has two small border crossings: one at Sasabe, just west of the Nogales area, and one at Lukeville–Sonoita. Lukeville has only a few residents, while Sonoita has a population of approximately 20,000—and the distinction of having been the only community in existence along the land border when the international dividing line was drawn in the 1850s. The Tohono O'odham (formerly Papago) Indian Reservation and the Organ Pipe National Monument take up a large part of Pima County.

Cochise County, Arizona–Agua Prieta, Naco, and Cananea, Sonora

Cochise County, with a population of approximately 90,000 (25 percent Mexican American), occupies the southeastern corner of Arizona and is a ranching, farming, and mining center. The U.S. towns that can be considered border communities are Douglas (pop. 14,000, 75 percent Mexican American), Bisbee (pop. 8,000), Naco (pop. 1,500), and Sierra Vista (pop. 35,000, 9 percent Mexican American). *Municipios* on the Mexican side of the border, all located in the state of Sonora, include Agua Prieta (pop. 50,000), adjacent to Douglas; Naco (pop. 5,000), contiguous with Naco, Arizona, and six miles south of Bisbee; and Cananea (pop. 22,000), approximately forty miles southwest of Naco.

The seat of Cochise County, Bisbee was once an important mining center. Now it serves as a weekend haven for Tucson residents. Douglas' economy, which previously depended upon the Phelps-Dodge copper smelter, relies on trade and commerce with Mexico. Naco, Arizona, remains a small community. Sierra Vista is the home of Fort Huachuca, a military intelligence center. This city has grown quite rapidly over the past twenty years, and now has more than twice the population of any other city in the county. No highway links Sierra Vista with the Mexican city of Cananea. Thus Cananea residents usually travel to Bisbee or Douglas when they want to visit the United States. Discussion continues regarding the possibility of a new highway connecting the two cities.

On the Mexican side, Agua Prieta has an economy that revolves around the *maquiladoras,* with more than one-third of its entire labor force employed in these factories. Cananea is still an important mining center. The mining community of Nacozari, located approximately sixty miles south of Douglas, also affects the border region. Not only does it depend upon trade and commerce with the United States, but the emissions from its copper smelter—along with emissions from smelters in Cananea and Douglas—have given the area the name of "the Gray Triangle."

In addition to the problem of air pollution, another issue for this area involves the water quality of the San Pedro River, which originates in Mexico and flows across the border just west of Naco. In the late 1970s and early 1980s, the river was polluted with heavy metals from mine wastes in Cananea, just fifteen miles south of the border. The problem was alleviated when Mexican officials diverted the flow south away from the border.

Border Focus Groups

BORDER ECOLOGY PROJECT

Established as a nonprofit organization in 1983, this advocacy group promotes joint U.S. and Mexican solutions to border environmental problems.

Border Ecology Project
P.O. Box 5
Naco, Arizona 85620
(602) 432-2688
Director: Richard Kamp

Tohono O'odham Tribal Council

The tribal council is the governing body for the Tohono O'odham nation (formerly referred to as Papagos), whose reservation occupies a portion of the borderlands northwest of Ambos Nogales.

Tohono O'odham Tribal Council
P.O. Box 837
Sells, Arizona 85634
(602) 383-2221

Ambos Nogales Area

Nogales, Arizona, and Nogales, Sonora (known as *Ambos,* or "both," Nogales), are located along the border sixty-five miles south of Tucson and 170 miles north of Hermosillo, the capital of Sonora. Founded in 1880, the two communities form one physical unit. They sit nestled in a narrow valley that is flanked by steep hills; only an artificial, arbitrarily positioned fence divides them. The Arizona community has grown modestly to its present population of 20,000 (approximately 85 percent Mexican American). In contrast, the Sonora side has experienced rapid growth since the early 1970s—in part due to the introduction of *maquiladoras*—and presently has a population estimated to be about 200,000.

Other than normal commercial activities, two industries are crucial to the Ambos Nogales area: *maquiladoras* and vegetable imports. Nogales, Sonora, is one of the most important centers for *maquiladoras,* with seventy plants and 20,000 employees. Nogales, Arizona, is the largest port of entry into the United States for fresh vegetables. Grown mainly along Mexico's west coast, almost two billion pounds of vegetables such as tomatoes, green peppers, cucumbers, and eggplants were imported into the United States at Nogales during the 1987–88 season, mostly between November and May.

Flood control and sewage disposal for the area have long been provided through the International Boundary and Water Commission. Despite recent improvements, these continue to present problems. Another important issue is air pollution caused by trash burning on the Mexican side of the border.

Due to its location on the main north-south highway connecting the western United States and Mexico, the Ambos Nogales area is a site of frequent contraband traffic. The data on this traffic is limited, of course.

Border Focus Groups

Ambos Nogales Commission / Comisión de los Ambos Nogales

The Ambos Nogales Commission was formed in the mid-1970s by the mayor of Nogales, Arizona, and the *presidente municipal* of Nogales, Sonora. It meets five or six times a year to discuss issues of mutual concern to the binational community.

Ambos Nogales Commission
City Hall Bldg.
1018 Grand Avenue
Nogales, Arizona 85621
(602) 287-6571, ext. 45

Comisión de los Ambos Nogales
Avenida Obregón y Calle Dr. Flores
 Guerra
84000 Nogales, Sonora
Tel. 2-0512 or 2-0118

West Mexico Vegetable Distributors Association

The Distributors Association works to facilitate the flow of Mexican produce into the United States.

West Mexico Vegetable Distributors Association
P.O. Box 848
Nogales, Arizona 85628
(602) 287-2707

Yuma, Arizona–San Luis Río Colorado, Sonora

Yuma is located in southwestern Arizona on the Colorado River, which is also the Arizona–California border. The city lies about twenty-five miles north of the U.S.–Mexico boundary at San Luis Río Colorado, Sonora, and a few miles east of the Andrade, California–Algodones, Baja

California, crossing. Yuma has a population of 50,000 (approximately 27 percent Mexican American). Agriculture, tourism, and light industry are the area's principal economic activities. San Luis Río Colorado, with a population estimated at 200,000, is the center of an agricultural region that has grown rapidly in the past two decades. It is now the largest Sonoran border community, and the fourth largest city in the state. San Luis, Arizona (pop. 3,000), lies directly adjacent to San Luis Río Colorado.

Institutions of higher education in the area include Arizona Western College, a two-year school at Yuma, and the Universidad de San Luis Río Colorado in San Luis Río Colorado.

2.8   CALIFORNIA–BAJA CALIFORNIA BORDER REGION

Imperial and Mexicali Valleys

Situated between the coastal mountains and the Colorado River, this region, much of it below sea level, is an important agricultural region for both countries. The area was first settled in the early 1900s with the advent of irrigated agriculture. Water supply and water quality issues are major points of contention between the two countries in this region. Although legally resolved, the Colorado River salinity problem is still a source of great irritation, as is pollution of the New River, which originates in Mexico but flows into the United States.

On the U.S. side of the border lies Imperial Valley, an agricultural area with a population of 90,000 that includes the cities of Calexico and El Centro. On the Mexican side, the large urban area of Mexicali presses up against the farmlands of California, separated only by a chain-link fence. Mexicali (pop. 800,000), the capital of Baja California, is the only border city that is also a state capital. It serves as a marketing and supply center for the important agricultural region of the Mexicali Valley, and as a center for *maquiladoras*. Cross-border retail sales and international trade and commerce are vital to both sides of the border.

Mexican institutions of higher education in the region include the Universidad Autónoma de Baja California, the Centro de Enseñanza Técnica y Superior (CETYS), and a branch of the Colegio de la Frontera Norte in Mexicali. On the U.S. side are San Diego State University's Imperial Valley Campus in Calexico, and the two-year Imperial Valley College in Imperial, California.

San Diego, California–Tijuana, Baja California

The San Diego–Tijuana metropolitan area has experienced more change in the past ten years than any other area along the border. Manifestations of this change include the new border crossing at Otay Mesa and the rapidly growing number of *maquiladoras*. Recognizing Tijuana's importance to San Diego, in 1986 the city of San Diego created the Mayor's Office of Binational Affairs, and in 1987 the county of San Diego established the Department of Transborder Affairs. The academic communities' interest in Mexico and the border is exemplified by the opening of the Center for U.S.–Mexican Studies at the University of California, San Diego; the Colegio de la Frontera Norte in Tijuana; and the Institute for Regional Studies of the Californias at San Diego State University. Increased attention is also being devoted to border issues at the University of San Diego, and at the Universidad Autónoma de Baja California in Tijuana.

Although a total of 2.2 million people live in San Diego county, the city of San Diego has a population of just over one million (14.9 percent Hispanic). Its downtown is located twelve miles from the international boundary; it is linked to Tijuana by an efficient light rail transit line and by freeways. San Diego's city limits extend far south, however, including most of Otay Mesa and San Ysidro.

San Diego's economy benefits from the area's proximity to Mexico. Tourism, retail sales to Mexicans, spillover effects of Mexican *maquiladora* development, and import-export commerce between the two countries are significant components. But San Diego's economy primarily depends upon the electronics and aerospace industries, non-Mexican tourism, and the two-billion-dollar revenue generated by U.S. military installations in the county. San Diego's tourist attractions include the resorts in La Jolla, a zoo, Sea World, and the beaches.

Tijuana, one of Mexico's most populous cities, is located on the border, and has approximately one million inhabitants. Because of extremely rapid and mostly unplanned growth, the city faces several severe problems. These include an insufficient supply of potable water and inadequate sewage treatment facilities. Although the former was partly alleviated by the opening of the Tijuana River aqueduct in 1983, the sewage treatment problem has worsened as the city grows, and San Diego's agreement to treat a portion of Tijuana's sewage has become problematic. Tijuana also has problems common to most cities, such as lack of adequate housing and medical facilities. Nevertheless, Tijuana is a vibrant city, where construction appears continual, unemployment is low, and the cultural scene is dynamic. Tijuana's economy relies heavily upon international trade and commerce, the expanding *maquiladora* industry, and tourism from the United States.

More legal crossings from Mexico into the United States take place at Tijuana than at any other point on the border—there are approximately forty million such crossings each year. But Tijuana is also the preferred departure point for people seeking to enter the United States without proper documentation. The Border Patrol calls this area the "war zone" because so many people attempt to cross each night, trying to negotiate their way through the hills, canyons, and marshes, hoping to avoid groups of bandits, as well as the Border Patrol. The rate of apprehension of undocumented immigrants is the highest of any area along the border.

A second border crossing was opened at Otay Mesa in the mid-1980s, alleviating some of the pressure at the San Ysidro crossing located a few miles away.

Current discussions between the cities address such issues as the traffic flow at the border crossings, the Tijuana sewage disposal problem, and air pollution.

Thirty miles east of Tijuana is the municipality of Tecate, with a 1980 population of approximately 42,000.

Border Focus Groups

DEPARTMENT OF TRANSBORDER AFFAIRS

This agency was established in late 1987 to coordinate San Diego County programs focusing on the U.S.–Mexico international border and the Pacific Rim. The department is involved in research, planning, and the development of public policy for border-related issues. These include trade and economic development, health, the environment, and public services.

Department of Transborder Affairs
San Diego County Administration Center
1600 Pacific Highway, room 273
San Diego, California 92101
(619) 531-6489
Director: Augie Bareño

MAYOR'S OFFICE OF BINATIONAL AFFAIRS

Established in May 1986, this office maintains working relations with similar agencies in Mexico. In 1988 it arranged the first joint meeting of the city councils of San Diego and Tijuana. Among the issues of interest

25

are economic development, tourism, border environmental issues, exchange programs, and a border information network.

Mayor's Office of Binational Affairs
1200 Third Avenue, suite 724
San Diego, California 92101
(619) 533-3940
Director: Elsa Saxod

SAN DIEGO COUNTY AIR POLLUTION CONTROL DISTRICT (APCD)

This agency is concerned with achieving and maintaining air quality standards in San Diego County. The APCD established the Tijuana–San Diego Air Quality Project in the mid-1970s, and has worked with Mexican government officials (especially from SEDUE [Secretaría de Desarrollo Urbano y Ecología]) on a regular basis since that time.

San Diego County Air Pollution Control District
9150 Chesapeake Drive
San Diego, California 92123
(619) 694-3332

3 THE ROLE OF THE U.S. FEDERAL GOVERNMENT

3.1 OVERVIEW

Operating within the State Department's Office of Mexican Affairs, the U.S.–Mexico Border Affairs Office coordinates relations between U.S. agencies and their counterparts in Mexico. It works closely with Mexico's Dirección General de Fronteras (*see Chapter 4, section 2*). Also operating under State Department supervision is the International Boundary and Water Commission.

Other U.S. federal agencies directly involved in border affairs are the Department of Justice, through the Immigration and Naturalization Service (and its enforcement branch, the U.S. Border Patrol) and the Drug Enforcement Administration; the Treasury Department, through the U.S. Customs Service and the Bureau of Alcohol, Tobacco, and Firearms; and the Department of Agriculture, through the Animal and Plant Health Inspection Service and the Agricultural Marketing Service. In addition, the Department of Commerce deals with international trade matters, and the Department of Housing and Urban Development is involved in border planning issues. The Department of the Interior maintains an interest in the border region through the National Parks Service and the Bureau of Reclamation.

In recent years, the Environmental Protection Agency has assumed a higher profile in border affairs, and now administers border environmental projects. The Department of Transportation, the U.S. Coast Guard, and the General Services Administration are all involved in border crossings and bridge building. Through its offices in the U.S. embassy in Mexico City and the U.S. consulates in Tijuana and Monterrey, the U.S. Information Agency, known as USIS in Mexico, works with cultural and educational exchanges along the border.

In 1976 the Southwest Border Regional Commission (SWBRC) was created with federal funding in order to approach border issues from a regional perspective. It was designed to promote economic development in the thirty-six counties of Arizona, California, New Mexico, and Texas that border on Mexico. The SWBRC was charged with setting policy for the border region, preparing a regional economic development plan, and implementing projects. A federal co-chair worked with the state co-chair, which alternated between the four border state governors. The Southwest

Border Regional Commission ceased to exist on September 30, 1981, partly because of federal budget cuts. Some of the work of the SWBRC has been carried on by the Border Governors' Conference, which is discussed in Chapter 6, section 1. [*Note:* In 1988 there was discussion in the U.S. Congress of creating a multistate commission, the U.S.–Mexico Border Regional Commission, to study measures for relieving poverty on the U.S. side of the border. No mention was made in the discussion of the history of the Southwest Border Regional Commission.]

Binational Relations

Each U.S. administration has developed its own format for binational meetings. Under President Carter's administration (1977–81)—which corresponded to López Portillo's administration—the U.S.–Mexico Consultative Mechanism was utilized. Directed by the ambassador at large to Mexico, Robert Krueger, and the Department of State, it coordinated and monitored federal-level activities concerning Mexico. The Consultative Mechanism had eight working groups, one of which was the Border Working Group.

During the Reagan Administration (1981–89)—which corresponded to the administrations of López Portillo, de la Madrid, and Salinas de Gortari—the Consultative Mechanism was replaced by other binational institutional arrangements, as follows.

•*Presidential Meetings.* These meetings were scheduled approximately once a year and reviewed the full range of U.S.–Mexican relations. Each president was accompanied by members of his cabinet.

•*Binational Commission.* The U.S.–Mexico Binational Commission was a cabinet-level group chaired jointly by the U.S. secretary of state and Mexico's foreign affairs secretary. It met annually and helped set the agenda for the next Presidential Meeting.

•*Agreement on Border Environmental Cooperation.* Signed by both presidents in August 1983, this agreement created two national positions: the associate administrator for international activities of the U.S. Environmental Protection Agency, and the undersecretary for ecology in Mexico's Secretaría de Desarrollo Urbano y Ecología (*secretariat of urban development and ecology*). Working groups were established to examine the issues of water pollution, air pollution, and hazardous substances and toxic wastes.

•*Migration Working Groups.* U.S.–Mexico Working Groups on migration and consular affairs were established in 1987, following passage of the Immigration Reform and Control Act of 1986. Part of the Binational Commission, these groups addressed a wide range of migration and consular issues, particularly along the U.S.–Mexico border.

These consultative mechanisms have been expanded under the administrations of George Bush and Carlos Salinas de Gortari, and now meet quarterly. Under various agreements and memoranda of understanding, there are also formal consultative arrangements and programs on civil aviation; international bridges and border crossings; agricultural trade and plant genetics, agricultural diseases, and pests; natural disasters in the border area; housing and urban development; public health; fish and wildlife conservation; weather forecasting; geothermal, nuclear, and other energy research; and radio and TV broadcasting and communications. For details on these agreements contact the U.S. Department of State (*see next section*).

3.2 FEDERAL AGENCIES

These listings include the agencies' Washington offices and contact persons, and, in most cases, their regional offices dealing with border affairs. Hundreds of federal offices that affect border communities in some way are not listed here. For a more detailed listing, consult the *Federal Executive Directory* and the *Federal Regional Executive Directory*, both published serially by Carroll Publishing Company, Washington, D.C.

Department of Agriculture

AGRICULTURAL MARKETING SERVICE

Both the McAllen and Nogales offices listed below publish data concerning the types and amounts of agricultural commodities imported into the United States from Mexico.

Market News Branch
Fruit & Vegetable Division
Agricultural Marketing Service
2503 South Bldg.
(P.O. Box 96456)
Washington, D.C. 20090-6456
(202) 447-2754

Market News Branch
Fruit & Vegetable Division
U.S. Department of Agriculture
P.O. Box 2292
Nogales, Arizona 85621
(602) 281-0374

Market News Branch
Fruit & Vegetable Division
U.S. Department of Agriculture
1231 East Hackberry
McAllen, Texas 78501
(512) 682-2581

Animal and Plant Health Inspection Service

Administrator
Animal & Plant Health Inspection Service, Veterinary Services
6505 Belcrest Road
Hyattsville, Maryland 20782
(301) 447-5601

Plant Protection and Quarantine Programs

SOUTH CENTRAL REGION

South Central Regional Office
Plant Protection & Quarantine
  Programs
3505 Boca Chica Blvd., suite 360
Brownsville, Texas 78521-4065
(512) 548-2513

AREA I OFFICES

Area I, Plant Protection &
  Quarantine Programs
3505 Boca Chica Blvd., suite 321
Brownsville, Texas 78521-4065
(512) 548-2631

•Work Unit 5, Plant Protection
  & Quarantine Programs
Cordova Border Station
3600 East Paisano, room 172-A
El Paso, Texas 79905
(915) 534-6650

••Work Station, Plant Protection
  & Quarantine Programs
International Bridge
P.O. Box 1001
Presidio, Texas 79845
(915) 229-3643

•Work Unit 6, Plant Protection
  & Quarantine Programs
P.O. Box 1829
Harlingen, Texas 78551
(512) 427-8527

•Work Unit 9, Plant Protection
  & Quarantine Programs
Mexican Fruit Fly Rearing
Facility
Route 3, Box 1005
Edinburg, Texas 78539
(512) 580-7374

AREA II OFFICES

Area II, Plant Protection &
  Quarantine Programs
3505 Boca Chica Blvd., suite 321
Brownsville, Texas 78521-4065
(512) 548-2631

•Work Unit 1, Plant Protection
  & Quarantine Programs
U.S. Border Station
160 Garrison Street, room 101
Eagle Pass, Texas 78852
(512) 773-3726

••Work Station, Plant Protection
& Quarantine Programs
U.S. Border Inspection Station
International Bridge, room 135
Del Rio, Texas 78840
(512) 775-3028

•Work Unit 4, Plant Protection
& Quarantine Programs
P.O. Box 277
Laredo, Texas 78042-0277
(512) 726-2225

AREA III OFFICES

Area III, Plant Protection &
Quarantine Programs
3505 Boca Chica Blvd., suite 321
Brownsville, Texas 78521-4065
(512) 548-2532

•Work Unit 2, Plant Protection
& Quarantine Programs
1500 East Elizabeth & International Blvd., room 224
Brownsville, Texas 78520
(512) 548-2543

•Work Unit 4, Plant Protection
& Quarantine Programs
International Bridge
P.O. Drawer R
Hidalgo, Texas 78557
(512) 843-2552

•Work Unit 6, Plant Protection
& Quarantine Programs
Progreso International Bridge
Route 2, Box 600
Weslaco, Texas 78596
(512) 565-4292

•Work Unit 7, Plant Protection
& Quarantine Programs
P.O. Box 185
Roma, Texas 78584
(512) 849-1561

WESTERN REGION

Western Regional Office
Plant Protection & Quarantine
Programs
9580 Micron Avenue, suite 1
Sacramento, California 95827
(916) 551-3220

AREA III OFFICES

Area III, Plant Protection &
Quarantine Programs
9580 Micron Avenue, suite 1
Sacramento, California 95827
(916) 551-3220

•Work Unit 3, Plant Protection
   & Quarantine Programs
720 San Ysidro Blvd.
San Ysidro, California 92073
(619) 428-7333

•Work Unit 4, Plant Protection
   & Quarantine Programs
200 East First Street
Calexico, California 92231
(619) 357-1828

•Work Unit 8, Plant Protection
   & Quarantine Programs
102 Terrace Avenue, room 116
Nogales, Arizona 85621
(602) 287-4783

••Work Station, Plant Protection
   & Quarantine Programs
5 Pan American Avenue
Douglas, Arizona 85607
(602) 364-7376

••Work Station, Plant Protection
   & Quarantine Programs
U.S. Border Station
P.O. Box 37
San Luis, Arizona 85349
(602) 627-2836

Department of Commerce

INTERNATIONAL TRADE ADMINISTRATION

Mexico Division
Mexico & Caribbean Basin Office
International Trade Administration
Fourth & Constitution Avenue, NW
Washington, D.C. 20230
(202) 377-4464

Foreign Commercial Service
American Embassy
Paseo de la Reforma 305
Colonia Cuauhtémoc
06500 México, D.F.
Tel. 211-0042
•*U.S. mailing address:*
  P.O. Box 3087
  Laredo, Texas 78044-3087

United States Trade Center
Liverpool 31
Colonia Juárez
06600 México, D.F.
Tel. 591-0155
•*U.S. mailing address:*
  P.O. Box 3087
  Laredo, Texas 78044-3087

Department of Housing and Urban Development (HUD)

Director, International Affairs
Department of Housing & Urban Development
451 Seventh Street, SW
Washington, D.C. 20410
(202) 755-5770

Department of the Interior

National Park Service
Big Bend Nat'l Park, Texas 79834
(915) 477-2251

National Park Service
Chamizal National Memorial
700 East San Antonio Street
El Paso, Texas 79901
(915) 543-6277

Department of Justice

DRUG ENFORCEMENT ADMINISTRATION (DEA)

Administrator
Drug Enforcement Administration
1405 Eye Street, NW
Washington, D.C. 20537
(202) 633-1337

REGIONAL OFFICES

Drug Enforcement Administration
[Texas]
1880 Regal Row
Dallas, Texas 75235
(214) 767-7151

Drug Enforcement Administration
[New Mexico]
316 U.S. Customs House
Denver, Colorado 80201
(303) 844-3951

Drug Enforcement Administration
[Arizona & California]
350 South Figueroa
Los Angeles, California 90071
(213) 894-2650

IMMIGRATION AND NATURALIZATION SERVICE (INS)

The INS is charged with regulating the entry of persons into the United
States, and enforcing immigration law; its enforcement branch is the U.S.
Border Patrol. Two regional offices and five district offices of the INS
oversee the U.S.–Mexico border region. Nine sector offices of the Border
Patrol administer its operations along the border. At each border cross-
ing there is a "port director" in charge of the local INS office.

Commissioner
Immigration & Naturalization Service
425 Eye Street, NW
Washington, D.C. 20536
(202) 633-1900

SOUTHERN REGION
(includes Texas & New Mexico)

Commissioner, Southern Region
Immigration & Naturalization
  Service
311 North Stimmons Freeway
Dallas, Texas 75207
(214) 767-6001

DISTRICT OFFICES

Harlingen District Director
Immigration & Naturalization
  Service
2102 Teege
Harlingen, Texas 78552
(512) 427-8592

San Antonio District Director
Immigration & Naturalization
  Service
727 East Durango
San Antonio, Texas 78206
(512) 229-6356

El Paso District Director
Immigration & Naturalization
  Service
Federal Bldg., suite B-214
700 East San Antonio Street
El Paso, Texas 79901
(915) 534-6634

INS Port Director
Gateway Bridge, room 2120
Brownsville, Texas 78520
(512) 546-1675

INS Port Director
Progreso, Texas 78579
(512) 565-6304

INS Port Director
Bridge Street
Hidalgo, Texas 78557
(512) 843-2201

INS Port Director
Rio Grande City, Texas 78582
(512) 487-2200

INS Port Director
Roma, Texas 78584
(512) 849-1676

INS Port Director
International Bridge
Laredo, Texas 78040
(512) 722-2484

INS Port Director
P.O. Box 4280
Eagle Pass, Texas 78852
(512) 773-9205

INS Port Director
P.O. Drawer G
Del Rio, Texas 78840
(512) 775-7528

•Del Rio Suboffice
 Amistad Border Crossing
 Amistad Dam, Texas 78841
 (512) 775-7213

INS Port Director
P.O. Box 9398
El Paso, Texas 79984
(915) 534-6762 / Americas Bridge
(915) 534-6771 / Del Norte Bridge
(915) 541-7366 / Ysleta Bridge

INS Port Director
Columbus, New Mexico 88029
(505) 531-2688

BORDER PATROL SECTORS

McAllen Sector, Border Patrol
2301 South Main Street
McAllen, Texas 78503
(512) 686-5496

Laredo Sector, Border Patrol
207 West Del Mar Blvd.
Laredo, Texas 78041
(512) 723-8197

Del Rio Sector, Border Patrol
P.O. Box 2020
Del Rio, Texas 78841
(512) 774-4681

Marfa Sector, Border Patrol
300 Madrid Street
Marfa, Texas 79843
(915) 729-4353

El Paso Sector, Border Patrol
8901 Montana Avenue
El Paso, Texas 79925
(915) 541-7850

WESTERN REGION
(includes Arizona & California)

Commissioner, Western Region
Immigration & Naturalization
 Service
24000 Avila Road
Laguna Niguel, California 92677
(714) 643-4236

DISTRICT OFFICES

Phoenix District Director
Immigration & Naturalization
 Service
230 North First Avenue
Phoenix, Arizona 85205
(602) 261-3122

San Diego District Director
Immigration & Naturalization
 Service
880 Front Street
San Diego, California 92188
(619) 557-5645

PORT DIRECTORS

INS Port Director
First & Pan American
Douglas, Arizona 85607
[includes Naco]
(602) 364-5532

INS Port Director
Grand Avenue P.O.E.
Border Inspection Station
Nogales, Arizona 85621
(602) 287-3609

INS Port Director
P.O. Box 448
San Luis, Arizona 85349
[includes Lukeville]
(602) 627-8816

INS Port Director
235 Andrade Road
Winter Haven, California 92283
(619) 572-0565

INS Port Director
200 East First Street
Calexico, California 92231
(619) 357-1143

INS Port Director
P.O. Box 219
Tecate, California 92080
(619) 557-5241

INS Port Director
720 East San Ysidro Blvd.
San Ysidro, California 92073
[includes Otay Mesa]
(619) 428-7311

BORDER PATROL SECTORS

Tucson Sector, Border Patrol
1970 West Ajo Way
Tucson, Arizona 85713
(602) 629-6871

Yuma Sector, Border Patrol
350 First Street
Yuma, Arizona 85364
(602) 782-9548

El Centro Sector, Border Patrol
1111 North Imperial Avenue
El Centro, California 92243
(619) 557-5645

San Diego Sector, Border Patrol
3752 East Beyer Blvd.
San Diego, California 92073
(619) 428-7251

Department of State

Office of Mexican Affairs
Department of State
2201 C Street
Washington, D.C. 20520
(202) 647-9894

International Boundary & Water
  Commission
Department of State
2201 C Street
Washington, D.C. 20520
(202) 647-8529

Department of Transportation

Federal Highway Administration

Administrator
Federal Highway Administration
400 Seventh Street, SW
Washington, D.C. 20590
(202) 366-0650

Department of the Treasury

Bureau of Alcohol, Tobacco, and Firearms

Director
Bureau of Alcohol, Tobacco, & Firearms
1200 Pennsylvania Avenue, NW
Washington, D.C. 20226
(202) 566-7511

Director, Southwest Region
[includes New Mexico & Texas]
Bureau of Alcohol, Tobacco, &
  Firearms
1114 Commerce, 7th floor
Dallas, Texas 75242
(214) 767-2280

Director, Western Region
[includes Arizona & California]
Bureau of Alcohol, Tobacco, &
  Firearms
221 Main Street, 11th floor
San Francisco, California 94105
(415) 974-9616

UNITED STATES CUSTOMS SERVICE

Commissioner
U.S. Customs Service
1301 Constitution Avenue, NW
Washington, D.C. 20229
(202) 566-2101

SOUTHWEST REGION
(includes Texas, New Mexico, & Arizona)

Commissioner, Southwest Region
U.S. Customs Service
5850 San Felipe, suite 500
Houston, Texas 77057
(713) 953-6843

DISTRICT OFFICES

Laredo District Director
U.S. Customs Service
Juárez–Lincoln Bridge, bldg. 2
Laredo, Texas 78044
(512) 726-2267

Nogales District Director
U.S. Customs Service
International & Terrace
Nogales, Arizona 85621
(602) 287-3637

PORT DIRECTORS

U.S. Customs Port Director
Gateway Bridge Office
Brownsville, Texas 78520
(512) 542-4232

U.S. Customs Port Director
Progreso, Texas 78579
(512) 565-6351

U.S. Customs Port Director
Bridge Street
Hidalgo, Texas 78557
(512) 843-2231

U.S. Customs Port Director
Rio Grande City, Texas
(512) 487-3498

U.S. Customs Port Director
Roma, Texas 78584
(512) 849-1818

U.S. Customs Port Director
P.O. Box 3130
Laredo, Texas 78044
(512) 726-2267

U.S. Customs Port Director
160 Garrison Street
Eagle Pass, Texas 78852
(512) 773-9454

U.S. Customs Port Director
H.C.R. no. 2, Box 23
Del Rio, Texas 78840
(512) 775-8502

U.S. Customs Port Director
P.O. Box 927
Presidio, Texas 79845
(915) 229-3961

U.S. Customs Port Director
P.O. Box 9516
El Paso, Texas 79985
(915) 534-6794 / Americas Bridge
(915) 534-6837 / Del Norte Bridge
(915) 534-6842 / Ysleta Bridge

U.S. Customs Port Director
P.O. Box 9
Columbus, New Mexico 88029
(505) 531-2686

U.S. Customs Port Director
First & Pan American
Douglas, Arizona 85607
(602) 364-8486

U.S. Customs Port Director
Terrace & International
Nogales, Arizona 85621
(602) 287-4955

U.S. Customs Port Director
P.O. Box H
San Luis, Arizona 85349
(602) 627-8854

PACIFIC REGION
(includes California)

Commissioner, Pacific Region
U.S. Customs Service
P.O. Box 2071
Los Angeles, California 90053
(213) 894-5900

DISTRICT OFFICE

San Diego District Director
U.S. Customs Service
880 Front Street, room 5-S-9
San Diego, California 92188
(619) 293-5360

U.S. Customs Port Director
235 Andrade Road
Winter Haven, California 92283
(619) 572-0089

U.S. Customs Port Director
200 East First Street
Calexico, California 92231
(619) 357-1195

U.S. Customs Port Director
1100 Paseo Internacional
San Ysidro, California 92073
[Otay Mesa]
(619) 428-7283

U.S. Customs Port Director
720 East San Ysidro Blvd.
San Ysidro, California 92073
(619) 428-7201

Environmental Protection Agency (EPA)

The EPA has been involved in border-related issues since the late 1970s, when Mexico and the United States signed a Memorandum of Understanding calling for the cooperative resolution of border environmental problems. Its role was expanded in 1983 with the signing by U.S. and Mexican presidents of an agreement on border environmental cooperation. Working with its counterpart in Mexico, the Secretaría de Desarrollo Urbano y Ecología (SEDUE), the EPA participates in working groups on water pollution, air pollution, and hazardous substances and toxic waste.

Associate Administrator, International Activities
Environmental Protection Agency
401 M Street, SW
Washington, D.C. 20460
(202) 382-4870

Administrator, Region VI
[includes New Mexico & Texas]
Environmental Protection Agency
Interstate Bank Tower
1445 Ross Avenue
Dallas, Texas 75202
(214) 655-2100

Administrator, Region IX
[includes Arizona & California]
Environmental Protection Agency
215 Fremont Street
San Francisco, California 94105
(415) 974-8153

General Services Administration (GSA)

The Public Building Service division of the GSA maintains and operates the bridges between the United States and Mexico. (*For further information on bridges, see Appendix 6.*)

Public Building Service
Eighteenth & F Streets, NW
Washington, D.C. 20405
(202) 566-1100

International Boundary and Water Commission, United States and Mexico (IBWC) / Comisión Internacional de Límites y Aguas, México y los Estados Unidos (CILA)

This binational commission is responsible for boundary demarcation, division of water resources, flood control, and other water-related issues of concern to the two nations. Both commissioners operate under the supervision of their respective foreign affairs departments. The U.S. section coordinates its activities with other federal, state, and municipal agencies, while the Mexican section works most closely with the secretary of agriculture and water resources. The two commissioners and their secretaries meet on a regular basis (at least once a week). In addition to its main offices in El Paso and Ciudad Juárcz, the IBWC maintains offices in San Diego, Yuma, Presidio, Laredo, and Harlingen, and at Amistad Dam (near Del Rio) and Falcon Dam (below Laredo). CILA has regional offices in Mexicali, Ciudad Acuña, and Nuevo Laredo, and at Anzaldúas Dam (near Reynosa).

International Boundary & Water Commission,
  United States & Mexico
The Commons, bldg. C, suite 310
4171 North Mesa Street
El Paso, Texas 79902
(915) 534-6700
Commissioner: Narendra N. Gunaji
Secretary: Robert M. Ybarra

Comisión Internacional de Límites y Aguas,
  México y los Estados Unidos
Avenida Universidad 2180
32320 Ciudad Juárez, Chihuahua
Tel. 13-7311
Commissioner: Carlos Santibáñez Mata
Secretary: Javier González Toussaint

3.3 FEDERAL LEGISLATORS FROM BORDER STATES

The addresses and phone numbers listed below are for the Washington offices. For information concerning offices in the legislator's home state or district, consult the *Federal Regional Executive Directory*.

Arizona

SENATE

Sen. Dennis DeConcini [D]
328 Hart Senate Office Bldg.
Washington, D.C. 20510
(202) 224-4521

Sen. John McCain [R]
111 Russell Senate Office Bldg.
Washington, D.C. 20510
(202) 224-2235

HOUSE OF REPRESENTATIVES

2nd District
Rep. Ed Pastor [D]
235 Cannon House Office Bldg.
Washington, D.C. 20515
(202) 225-4065

5th District
Rep. James Kolbe [R]
1222 Longworth House Office Bldg.
Washington, D.C. 20515
(202) 225-2542

California

SENATE

Sen. Alan Cranston [D]
112 Hart Senate Office Bldg.
Washington, D.C. 20510
(202) 224-3553

Sen. John Seymour [R]
902 Hart Senate Office Bldg.
Washington, D.C. 20510
(202) 224-3841

HOUSE OF REPRESENTATIVES

45th District
Rep. Duncan Hunter [R]
133 Cannon House Office Bldg.
Washington, D.C. 20515
(202) 225 5672

New Mexico

SENATE

Sen. Jeff Bingaman [D]
502 Hart Senate Office Bldg.
Washington, D.C. 20510
(202) 224-5521

Sen. Peter Domenici [R]
434 Dirksen Senate Office Bldg.
Washington, D.C. 20510
(202) 224-6621

HOUSE OF REPRESENTATIVES

2nd District
Rep. Joseph R. Skeen [R]
1007 Longworth House Office Bldg.
Washington, D.C. 20515
(202) 225-2365

Texas

SENATE

Sen. Lloyd Bentsen [D]
703 Hart Senate Office Bldg.
Washington, D.C. 20510
(202) 224-5922

Sen. Phil Gramm [R]
370 Russell Senate Office Bldg.
Washington, D.C. 20510
(202) 224-2934

HOUSE OF REPRESENTATIVES

15th District
Rep. Kika de la Garza [D]
1401 Longworth House Office Bldg.
Washington, D.C. 20515
(202) 225-2531

21st District
Rep. Lamar Smith [R]
509 Cannon House Office Bldg.
Washington, D.C. 20515
(202) 225-4236

16th District
Rep. Ronald Coleman [D]
416 Cannon House Office Bldg.
Washington, D.C. 20515
(202) 225-4831

23rd District
Rep. Albert Bustamante [D]
1113 Longworth House Office Bldg.
Washington, D.C. 20515
(202) 225-4511

Congressional Border Caucus

Formed in 1983, the Congressional Border Caucus is a bipartisan group that meets twice a month. Composed of members whose districts are located in or adjacent to the U.S.–Mexico border region, the caucus has sought to provide a forum for increasing national awareness of the unique problems and issues facing the borderlands.

Congressional Border Caucus
U.S. House of Representatives
Washington, D.C. 20515

4 THE ROLE OF THE MEXICAN FEDERAL GOVERNMENT

The Mexican federal agencies most directly involved in border issues are the Secretaría de Relaciones Exteriores, especially through the Dirección General de Fronteras, the Mexican section of the International Boundary and Water Commission, and the Dirección General para América del Norte; the Secretaría de Gobernación, through the Dirección General de Servicios Migratorios; the Secretaría de Hacienda y Crédito Público; the Secretaría de Programación y Presupuesto; the Secretaría de Comunicaciones y Transportes and its Caminos y Puentes Federales de Ingresos y Servicios Conexos; the Secretaría de Desarrollo Urbano y Ecología; and the Secretaría de Comercio y Fomento Industrial.

Several interdepartmental working groups currently deal with border affairs, and meet regularly with their U.S. counterparts. One example is the working group on bridges and international crossings, which includes representatives from most of the agencies named above, plus a representative from Ferrocarriles Nacionales de México, the national railroad.

During the past thirty years, the Mexican government has developed bureaucratic mechanisms in its efforts to respond to the unique needs of the border region. Although some are inactive, these mechanisms are described below in order to give a sense of the recent history—and future possibilities—of Mexican government border policy.

Programa Nacional Fronterizo (PRONAF)
(*national border program*)

This Mexican government initiative, lasting from 1961 to 1965, sought to improve the infrastructure of the border communities. Through the creation of parks, shopping centers, and cultural centers, PRONAF succeeded in improving the public image of those cities. But it did not—nor was it primarily intended to—address the long-range issue of their economic development.

Programa de la Industria Maquiladora
(Border Industrialization Program [BIP])

Created in 1965, BIP provides the basic framework for the establishment of in-bond plants—the *maquiladoras*—in Mexican border communities. For more detail, see Chapter 7, section 1.

Comisión Intersecretarial para el Fomento de la Franja Fronteriza Norte y Perímetros Libres
(*intersecretarial commission for the development of the northern border area and free zones*)

The intersecretarial commission was created in 1972 for the purpose of conducting studies and formulating programs that stimulate economic development in the border region, and accelerate its economic integration with the rest of Mexico. It included representatives from the secretariats of commerce and industrial development, finance, and agriculture.

Comisión Coordinadora del Programa de Desarrollo de las Franjas Fronterizas y Zonas Libres (CODEF)
(*coordinating commission of the program for development of border areas and free zones*)

Established in 1977 by the Mexican government, CODEF was charged with spearheading a national "border development program." It was supposed to coordinate decision making among federal agencies in matters of economic and social policy pertaining to border regions and free zones. It was based in the Secretaría de Programación y Presupuesto, and included members from other *secretarías:* Hacienda y Crédito Público, Comercio, Agricultura y Recursos Hidráulicos, Asentamientos Humanos y Obras Públicas, Trabajo y Previsión Social, and Turismo. CODEF ceased functioning in 1982.

Comisión Legislativa de Asuntos Fronterizos
(legislative commission on border affairs)

The Mexican Cámara de Diputados (chamber of deputies, roughly equivalent to the U.S. House of Representatives) maintains a committee concerned with border issues.

Diputado Víctor Hugo Celaya Celaya
Comisión Legislativa de Asuntos Fronterizos
Palacio Legislativo
San Lázaro
06019 México, D.F.
Tel. 795-5188, ext. 1335, or 795-7044, ext. 254

4.2   EXECUTIVE DEPARTMENTS

The heads of the executive departments, known by the rank of cabinet minister, are appointed and serve at the will of the president. They frequently represent the different factions within the ruling party, the PRI (Partido Revolucionario Institucional [*institutional revolutionary party*]), which has ruled the Mexican political system since it was founded in the 1920s.

Note: The great Mexico City earthquake of 1985 destroyed or damaged many downtown buildings, causing many agencies to be moved to provisional offices. Therefore, the likelihood of error in the Mexico City addresses listed below is greater than would otherwise be the case.

Procuraduría General de la República
(*attorney general's office*)

This agency is responsible for the prosecution of all federal crimes. Recently, under former president Miguel de la Madrid's administration, it was directed to take the lead in the nation's drug-fighting effort.

Procuraduría General de la República
Soto 81
Colonia Guerrero
06300 México, D.F.
Tel. 529-2822 or 529-2802

Secretaría de Agricultura y Recursos Hidráulicos (SARH)
(*secretariat of agriculture and water resources*)

SARH plans and regulates production in the agricultural, livestock, and forestry industries, and also administers federal forest preserves. It

operates schools and experimental institutes of agriculture, animal hus-
bandry, and forestry. SARH is responsible for overseeing the construction of irrigation projects, managing the national irrigation system, and
assigning water rights and concessions to small towns and villages.

Secretaría de Agricultura y Recursos Hidráulicos
Insurgentes Sur 476, 13º piso
Colonia Roma Sur
06760 México, D.F.
Tel. 584-0096 or 584-0271

Secretaría de Comercio y Fomento Industrial (SECOFI)
(secretariat of commerce and industrial development)

SECOFI is charged with formulating and implementing national policy
for industry and commerce. It regulates the commercialization and dis-
tribution of goods and services, encourages the development of private
industry, assists in the export of manufactured goods, and promotes foreign trade. Through the Subdirección de la Industria Maquiladora y
Desarrollo Regional, it approves and monitors the operations of the
maquiladoras along the U.S.–Mexico border.

Secretaría de Comercio y Fomento Industrial
Alfonso Reyes 30, 10º piso
Colonia Condesa
06140 México, D.F.
Tel. 286-1483 or 286-1823

DIRECCIÓN DEL REGISTRO NACIONAL DE INVERSIONES EXTRANJERAS
(office of the national registry of foreign investments)

Dirección del Registro Nacional de Inversiones Extranjeras
Monte Elbruz 132, 6º piso
Colonia Lomas de Chapultepec
01100 México, D.F.
Tel. 520-4724

Subdirección de la Industria Maquiladora y Desarrollo Regional
(suboffice of the maquiladora industry and regional development)

Subdirección de la Industria Maquiladora y Desarrollo Regional
Periférico Sur 3025
Colonia Héroes de Padierna
10700 México, D.F.
Tel. 683-3918 or 683-4394

SECOFI REGIONAL OFFICES

SECOFI
Avenida Lauro Villar 198-A,
  1ᵉʳ piso
Colonia Las Palmas
87420 Matamoros, Tamaulipas
Tel. 3-5467 or 3-5259

SECOFI
Bulevar Hidalgo 1090, Poniente
Colonia Longoria
88660 Reynosa, Tamaulipas
Tel. 3-7561 or 3-7614

SECOFI
Avenida Guerrero 2902
88240 Nuevo Laredo, Tamaulipas
Tel. 4-0196 or 4-0303

SECOFI
Morelos 211
26000 Piedras Negras, Coahuila
Tel. 2-2441 or 2-2642

SECOFI
Tomás Alba Edison y Malecón 1510
32310 Ciudad Juárez, Chihuahua
Tel. 6-6752 or 6-7562

SECOFI
Avenida Alvaro Obregón y Manuel
  González 360, altos
84000 Nogales, Sonora
Tel. 2-6858 or 2-3147

SECOFI
Palacio Federal, nivel 2, cuerpo A
Centro Cívico y Comercial de
  Mexicali
21000 Mexicali, Baja California
Tel. 57-4273 or 57-4891

SECOFI
Calle Sexta y Ocampo, no. 2241
22000 Tijuana, Baja California
Tel. 85-0552 or 85-1621

Secretaría de Comunicaciones y Transportes (SCT)
(*secretariat of communications and transportation*)

This agency manages communications and transportation policy. It administers the national mail system, and oversees electric and electronic communications. It also grants concessions for airline services and issues permits for the establishment of federal highway transportation routes (including international bridges).

Secretaría de Comunicaciones y Transportes
Cuerpo C, 1ᵉʳ piso
Xola y Avenida Universidad
Colonia Narvarte
03028 México, D.F.
Tel. 530-7640 or 519-1319

CAMINOS Y PUENTES FEDERALES DE INGRESOS Y SERVICIOS CONEXOS
(*federal toll roads and bridges and related services*)

Caminos y Puentes Federales de Ingresos y Servicios Conexos
Avenida Plan de Ayala 629
Colonia Lomas del Mirador
62180 Cuernavaca, Morelos
Tel. 15-6100 or 15-6122

Secretaría de Desarrollo Urbano y Ecología (SEDUE)
(*secretariat of urban development and ecology*)

Among SEDUE's primary responsibilities is the formulation of policy for city-planning, housing, and ecological issues. It promotes research related to these subjects, and also assists *ejidos* (government-sponsored communal farms) in securing housing and building materials. In recent years, through the Dirección General de Ecología, it has become the lead agency in establishing clean-air statutes. SEDUE operates pollution monitoring stations in the Distrito Federal and throughout the country. (*See "Environmental Protection Agency" in Chapter 3, section 2, for a description of the joint presidential decree on border environmental issues that is administered by both SEDUE and the EPA.)*

Secretaría de Desarrollo Urbano y Ecología
Edificio B, PA
Constituyentes 947
Colonia Belén de las Flores
01110 México, D.F.
Tel. 271-2844 or 271-1441

DIRECCIÓN GENERAL DE ECOLOGÍA
(general office of ecology)

Dirección General de Ecología
Río Elba 20
Colonia Cuautémoc
06500 México, D.F.
Tel. 553-6286

Secretaría de Gobernación
(secretariat of the interior)

This secretariat is the largest and most politically important of all the executive departments. The agency's broad-based responsibilities include the policing of internal and external security, making it similar to a combination of the U.S.'s Federal Bureau of Investigation and Central Intelligence Agency. It organizes and oversees all federal elections, and sets the government's official calendar. It also monitors the radio, television, film, and publishing industries, and formulates population policy. Gobernación's Dirección General de Servicios Migratorios administers regulations concerning foreign nationals living in Mexico.

Secretaría de Gobernación
Bucareli 99, 1ᵉʳ piso
Colonia Juárez
06699 México, D.F.
Tel. 566-0245 or 566-0262

Dirección General de Servicios Migratorios
(general office of immigration services)

Dirección General de Servicios Migratorios
Albañiles 19
Colonia Penitenciaría
15350 México, D.F.
Tel. 795-2177 or 795-6724

PORT-OF-ENTRY OFFICES

Oficina de Migración
87380 Matamoros, Tamaulipas
Tel. 2-0251 or 2-3457

Jefe de Población
Garita Juárez
88780 Reynosa, Tamaulipas
Tel. 2-1312

Delegado de Servicios Migratorios
Avenida 15 de Junio y Guerrero
88000 Nuevo Laredo, Tamaulipas
Tel. 2-2171

Oficina de Población
Terán y Ocampo
26000 Piedras Negras, Coahuila
Tel. 2-0030

Jefe de Población
Puerta de México
26200 Ciudad Acuña, Coahuila
Tel. 2-1052

Oficina de Población
32880 Ojinaga, Chihuahua

Servicios Migratorios
Avenida Lerdo y Malecón
32000 Ciudad Juárez, Chihuahua
Tel. 15-0497 or 15-1024

Oficina de Migración
31830 General Rodrigo Quevedo,
  Chihuahua
Tel. 6-0155

Jefe de Población
Aduana Fronteriza
84200 Agua Prieta, Sonora

Oficina de Migración
Puerta de México
84000 Nogales, Sonora
Tel. 2-0026

Oficina de Población
Aduana Fronteriza
84300 San Luis Río Colorado,
  Sonora

Delegado de Servicios Migratorios
Puerta de México
Línea Internacional
21000 Mexicali, Baja California
Tel. 52-6993 or 52-9050

Subdelegación de Servicios
  Migratorios
Garita Internacional
21400 Tecate, Baja California
Tel. 4-1249

Subdelegación de Servicios
  Migratorios
Garita Internacional
Mesa de Otay
22390 Tijuana, Baja California
Tel. 23-3860

Delegado de Servicios Migratorios
Puerta de México
Garita Internacional
22000 Tijuana, Baja California
Tel. 82-4947

Secretaría de Hacienda y Crédito Público
(*secretariat of the treasury and public finance*)

This agency develops the federal government's budget, proposes tax legislation, and collects all federal taxes. It also sets monetary and public-credit policy. In addition, it administers the national banking system, and controls the insurance, securities, and bonds industries. Hacienda oversees the federal fiscal police and the Dirección General de Aduanas, which includes the border customs posts.

Secretaría de Hacienda y Crédito Público
Palacio Nacional
06060 México, D.F.
Tel. 518-5420

DIRECCIÓN GENERAL DE ADUANAS
(*general customs office*)

Dirección General de Aduanas
Departamento de Regímenes Temporales
Avenida 20 de Noviembre 195, 6º piso
Colonia Centro
06067 México, D.F.
Tel. 709-6068 or 709-6185

BORDER CUSTOMS POSTS

Administrador de Aduana
Calle Catorce y Galeana
87380 Matamoros, Tamaulipas
Tel. 2-3639

Aduana Fronteriza
88810 Nuevo Progreso, Tamaulipas

Administrador de Aduana
Avenida Miguel Alemán s/n
88780 Reynosa, Tamaulipas
Tel. 2-0537 or 2-0538

Administrador de Aduana
Antiaga y César López de Lara
88000 Nuevo Laredo, Tamaulipas

Administrador de Aduana
Zaragoza y Fuente
26000 Piedras Negras, Coahuila
Tel. 2-0199

Administrador de Aduana
Madero y Matamoros
26200 Ciudad Acuña, Coahuila
Tel. 2-0077

Aduana Fronteriza
32880 Ojinaga, Chihuahua

Administrador de Aduana
32000 Ciudad Juárez, Chihuahua
Tel. 16-0936 or 16-0833

Aduana Fronteriza
31830 General Rodrigo Quevedo,
  Chihuahua
Tel. 6-0285

Aduana Fronteriza
Calle Primera y Avenida Tercera
84200 Agua Prieta, Sonora
Tel. 8-0283

Aduana Fronteriza
Garita 3
Línea Internacional
84000 Nogales, Sonora
Tel. 2-5457

Aduana Fronteriza
83400 San Luis Río Colorado,
  Sonora

Aduana Fronteriza
Bajos del Río Nuevo s/n
21000 Mexicali, Baja California
Tel. 52-9525 or 52-2974

Aduana Fronteriza
21400 Tecate, Baja California
Tel. 4-1151

Aduana Fronteriza
José María Larroque s/n
Colonia Federal
22310 Tijuana, Baja California
Tel. 83-1388

Secretaría de Programación y Presupuesto
(secretariat of planning and budget)

This agency is responsible for calculating projected federal expenditures, including those of the parastate industries. It monitors the federal government's spending programs, and organizes the financial accounts of all cabinet-level secretariats. Through the Instituto Nacional de Estadísticas, Geografía e Informática, it processes and publishes official statistics, including data on the *maquiladoras*.

Secretaría de Programación y Presupuesto
Patio de Honor
Palacio Nacional
06060 México, D.F.
Tel. 542-8761 or 542-8762

Instituto Nacional de Estadísticas, Geografía e Informática (INEGI)
(*national institute of statistics, geography, and data*)

Instituto Nacional de Estadísticas, Geografía e Informática
Torre A, PH
Patriotismo 711
Colonia Mixcoac
03910 México, D.F.
Tel. 598-8345 or 598-8241

Secretaría de Relaciones Exteriores
(*secretariat of foreign affairs*)

Charged with managing all foreign policy, this agency intervenes in any matters related to nationality, naturalization, and extradition. It concedes to foreigners licenses to acquire titles to land or other real estate. In the late 1980s, Relaciones Exteriores created the Dirección General de Fronteras to monitor border issues more closely. It is also in charge of the Dirección General para América del Norte and the Comisión Internacional de Límites y Agua (*see "International Boundary and Water Commission" in Chapter 3, section 2*). *Maquiladoras* with foreign capital must register for authorization with the *secretaría* through the Dirección General de Asuntos Jurídicos.

Secretaría de Relaciones Exteriores
Ricardo Flores Magón 1, 19º piso
Colonia Nonoalco Tlatelolco
06995 México, D.F.
Tel. 782-3935 or 782-3937

Dirección General de Asuntos Jurídicos
(general office for judicial affairs)

Dirección General de Asuntos Jurídicos
Ricardo Flores Magón 1, 1er piso
Colonia Nonoalco Tlatelolco
06995 México, D.F.
Tel. 782-3440 or 782-2714

Dirección General de Fronteras
(general office of borders)

Dirección General de Fronteras
Avenida Juárez 101, 25º piso
Colonia Tabacalera
06040 México, D.F.
Tel. 510-9414 or 254-8388, ext. 2969

Dirección General para América del Norte
(general office for North America)

Dirección General para América del Norte
Homero 213, 13º piso
Colonia Chapultepec Morales
11570 México, D.F.
Tel. 254-6639 or 254-6735

Secretaría de Turismo
(secretariat of tourism)

This agency formulates and oversees national tourism policy. In addition to promoting the development of a tourism infrastructure on both regional and national levels, it channels foreign investment in the Mexican tourism industry. Turismo governs all aspects of businesses serving tourists, including prices and tariffs. It also sponsors festivals of traditional folklore and culture.

Secretaría de Turismo
Presidente Masaryk 172, 3ᵉʳ piso
Colonia Bosques de Chapultepec
11587 México, D.F.
Tel. 250-5014 or 250-8555

Dirección General de Coordinaciones Regionales de Turismo
(*general office for the regional coordination of tourism*)

Dirección General de Coordinaciones Regionales de Turismo
Presidente Masaryk 172, 3ᵉʳ piso
Colonia Bosques de Chapultepec
11587 México, D.F.
Tel. 250-4298 or 250-8555, ext. 238

5 DIPLOMATIC REPRESENTATION

5.1 EMBASSIES

United States Embassy
Paseo de la Reforma 305
Colonia Cuautémoc
06500 México, D.F.
Tel. 211-0042
•U.S. mailing address:
 P.O. Box 3087
 Laredo, Texas 78044-3087

Embassy of Mexico
2829 Sixteenth Street
Washington, D.C. 20009
(202) 234-6000

5.2 CONSULATES

U.S. Consulates

U.S. Consulate
Avenida Primera 2002
(Apartado Postal 451)
87330 Matamoros, Tamaulipas
Tel. 2-5251
Telex 035827 ACMTME
•U.S. mailing address:
 P.O. Box 633
 Brownsville, Texas 78520-0633

U.S. Consulate
Calle Allende 3330
Colonia Jardín
(Apartado Postal 38)
88260 Nuevo Laredo, Tamaulipas
Tel. 4-0696
Telex 036849 ACMLME
•U.S. mailing address:
 P.O. Drawer 3089
 Laredo, Texas 78044-3089

U.S. Consulate General
Avenida Constitución 411, Poniente
(Apartado Postal 152)
64000 Monterrey, Nuevo León
Tel. 45-2120
Telex 0382853 ACMYME
•Cultural Affairs Office
 Tel. 42-36-40
•U.S. mailing address:
 P.O. Box 3098
 Laredo, Texas 78044-3098

U.S. Consulate General
López Mateos 924-N
(Apartado Postal 1681)
32000 Ciudad Juárez, Chihuahua
Tel. 13-4048
Telex 033840 AMCOMC
•U.S. mailing address:
 P.O. Box 10545
 El Paso, Texas 79995-0545

U.S. Consulate
Monterrey 133
(Apartado Postal 972)
83260 Hermosillo, Sonora
Tel. 7-2375 or 7-2382
Telex 058829 ACHEME
•U.S. mailing address:
 P.O. Box 3087
 Laredo, Texas 78044-3087

U.S. Consulate General
Tapachula 96
Colonia Hipódromo
Tijuana, Baja California
Tel. 81-7400
Telex 566836
•Border Affairs Office
 U.S. Information Service (USIS)
 Tel. 81-7654
•U.S. mailing address:
 P.O. Box 1538
 San Ysidro, California 92073

Mexican Consulates

Mexican Consulate
Elizabeth & East Seventh
Brownsville, Texas 78520
(512) 542-4431

Mexican Consulate
1418 Beach Street, suite 104
McAllen, Texas 78501
(512) 686-0243

Mexican Consulate General
127 Navarro Street
San Antonio, Texas 78205
(512) 227-9145

Mexican Consulate
1612 Farragut
Laredo, Texas 78040
(512) 723-6360

Mexican Consulate
140 Adams Street
Eagle Pass, Texas 78852
(512) 773-9255

Mexican Consulate
1010 South Main Street
Del Rio, Texas 78840
(512) 775-2352

Mexican Consulate
730 O'Reilly Street
Presidio, Texas 79845
(915) 229-3745

Mexican Consulate General
910 East San Antonio Street
El Paso, Texas 79901
(915) 533-3644

Mexican Consulate
855 Cochise
Douglas, Arizona 85607
(602) 364-2275

Mexican Consulate
137 Terrace Avenue, suite 150
Nogales, Arizona 85621
(602) 287-2521

Mexican Consulate
331–333 West Second Street
Calexico, California 92231
(619) 357-3863

Mexican Consulate General
610 A Street
San Diego, California 92101
(619) 231-8414

6 THE ROLE OF STATE GOVERNMENTS

6.1 OVERVIEW

Over the past decade, border states have become increasingly active in the search for solutions to regional problems. Their ability to take independent action is limited, however. The four states on the U.S. side of the border must share authority with federal, county, and city governments. On the Mexican side, the six border states share power with federal and municipal governments. (A Mexican *municipio* is roughly equivalent to a U.S. county, and its name is also the name of its seat.) Furthermore, due to the traditional dominance of the federal level in Mexican government, Mexican state policy has often been set by Mexico City. Despite such constraints on their authority, states on both sides of the border have begun to work directly with each other.

Border Governors' Conference

The Border Governors' Conference is an offshoot of the Southwest Border Regional Commission. Since 1980, the governors of the ten border states have met regularly to discuss issues of mutual interest. These meetings occur almost annually, and executive committee meetings of the governors' staffs take place two to three times each year. The Governors' Conference is establishing an information data bank on the border states to be based in Saltillo, Coahuila. For information on meetings of the conference, contact the office of any border state governor.

Binational Attorneys General Meeting

The attorneys general of the ten border states have met biannually since 1986 to review matters of mutual concern. Information concerning the next meeting can be obtained from the office of any of the ten attorneys general.

6.2 BORDER-STATE GOVERNORS

United States

Fife Symington [R]
Office of the Governor
1700 West Washington
Phoenix, Arizona 85007
(602) 542-4331

Pete Wilson [R]
Office of the Governor
State Capitol
Sacramento, California 95814
(916) 445-2841

Bruce King [D]
Office of the Governor
State Capitol
Santa Fe, New Mexico 87503
(505) 827-3000

Ann Richards [D]
Office of the Governor
State Capitol
Austin, Texas 78711
(512) 463-2000

Mexico

Ernesto Ruffo Appel
Palacio de Gobierno
Centro Cívico
Calzada Independencia y Héroes
21000 Mexicali, Baja California
Tel. 57-3000, 57-1190, or 57-1915

Fernando Baeza Meléndez
Palacio de Gobierno
Venustiano Carranza 815, 2º piso
31009 Chihuahua, Chihuahua

Eliseo Mendoza Berrueto
Palacio de Gobierno
Plaza de Armas, centro
25000 Saltillo, Coahuila
Tel. 4-5611 or 4-8375

Jorge Treviño Martínez
Palacio de Gobierno
5 de Mayo y Zaragoza
64009 Monterrey, Nuevo León

Rodolfo Félix Valdez
Palacio de Gobierno
Hidalgo s/n
83269 Hermosillo, Sonora
Tel. 2-0001 or 7-1161

Américo Villareal Guerra
Palacio de Gobierno
87009 Ciudad Victoria,
  Tamaulipas

6.3   STATE GOVERNMENT ORGANIZATIONS

United States

Arizona

ARIZONA–SONORA COMMISSION/COMISIÓN SONORA–ARIZONA

Founded in 1960, these cross-boundary commissions are designed to promote goodwill, understanding, and development of the two states. They attempt to formulate programs and to advise both public- and private-sector organizations. Committees are concerned with commerce and industry, public health, agriculture and livestock, tourism, art and culture, banking and finance, and legal issues. The Arizona–Sonora Commission publishes a quarterly newsletter, *The Cronista*.

Arizona–Sonora Commission
P.O. Box 13564
Phoenix, Arizona 85002
(602) 255-1345
Executive Director: Tony Certosimo

Comisión Sonora–Arizona
Palacio de Gobierno
Hidalgo s/n
83269 Hermosillo, Sonora

ARIZONA DEPARTMENT OF COMMERCE

The Community Development Office of the Arizona Department of Commerce publishes two-page community profiles of Arizona towns, including the border communities of Douglas, Nogales, San Luis, and Yuma. The International Trade Division assists Arizona companies that export to Mexico, and promotes job-creating foreign investment in Arizona. It publishes a number of guides and directories related to international trade.

Community Development Office
Arizona Department of Commerce
1700 West Washington
Phoenix, Arizona 85007
(602) 542-5434

International Trade Division
Arizona Department of Commerce
1700 West Washington
Phoenix, Arizona 85007
(602) 542-4927

California

GOVERNOR'S OFFICE ON CALIFORNIA–MEXICO AFFAIRS (OCMA)

This office was established in 1982 to serve as a source of information for the California legislature and state agencies, the business community, the U.S. State Department, and other federal agencies interested in Mexico. Located in the Governor's Office of Planning and Research, OCMA works with the Commission of the Californias and the Border Governors' Conference to foster productive economic and political relations between California and Mexico.

The Commission of the Californias, established in 1964, is composed of representatives of the states of California, Baja California, and Baja California Sur. The commission seeks to foster economic, social, and cultural ties among the three states. Since 1982, the California section has operated under the auspices of the Governor's Office on California–Mexico Affairs.

Governor's Office on California–Mexico Affairs
1400 Tenth Street
Sacramento, California 95814
(916) 322-4811
Director: Francisco Márquez

CALIFORNIA STATE OFFICE OF TRADE AND INVESTMENT IN MEXICO CITY

The California Office in Mexico City seeks to promote trade between California and Mexico, and to provide Californians with accurate trade and investment information. In addition to monitoring investment in the *maquiladora* industry, it attends to border relations between California and Mexico.

California State Office of Trade & Investment in Mexico City
Paseo de la Reforma 450, 4º piso
Colonia Juárez
06600 México, D.F.
Tel. 208-5161, 208-5641, or 208-5701
Director: Carlos Valderrama

New Mexico

NEW MEXICO BORDER COMMISSION (NMBC)

The NMBC was created in 1981 to foster a cordial and cooperative relationship between New Mexico, Chihuahua, and the Republic of Mexico. It attempts to facilitate the exchange of information between New Mexico and Chihuahua, for the purpose of enhancing the development of *maquiladoras*. The NMBC has also examined the feasibility of a border crossing between Santa Teresa or Anapra, New Mexico, and Ciudad Juárez.

New Mexico Border Commission
P.O. Box 3JBR
New Mexico State University
Las Cruces, New Mexico 88003
(505) 646-3524

Texas

Note: The Good Neighbor Commission of Texas ceased operations on August 31, 1987.

TEXAS–MEXICO AUTHORITY

This advisory board to the Texas Department of Commerce seeks to address problems in the commercial and industrial development of the Texas–Mexico border. The authority also advises other Texas state agencies, state universities, the Border Governors' Conference, and U.S. and Mexican federal authorities. It serves as the umbrella organization for the four Texas–Mexico commissions listed below. For further information, contact Tom Stellman, Border Development Coordinator.

Texas–Mexico Authority
Texas Department of Commerce
816 Congress Avenue, suite 1200
Austin, Texas 78701
(512) 320-9659
Mailing address:
  P.O. Box 12728
  Capitol Station
  Austin, Texas 78711

BI-STATE REGIONAL COMMISSIONS

Composed of fifteen members from each state, these commissions, listed below, examine the following topics: industrial development, trade, tourism, agriculture, education, and the environment. In addition to helping define specific priorities of the Texas–Mexico Authority, the Bi-State Commissions serve as the authority's working arm. Although the commissions have identical areas of interest, they each have region-specific projects. The address for these commissions is the same as that of the Texas–Mexico Authority.
•Texas–Chihuahua Bi-State Regional Commission
•Texas–Coahuila Bi-State Regional Commission
•Texas–Tamaulipas Bi-State Regional Commission
•Texas–Nuevo León Bi-State Regional Commission

GOVERNOR'S OFFICE OF IMMIGRATION AND REFUGEE AFFAIRS

This office was created to address issues pertaining to immigrants and refugees, and to assist these people with settlement in Texas.

Governor's Office of Immigration and Refugee Affairs
9101 Burnet Road, suite 216
Austin, Texas 78758
(512) 873-2400
Special Program Manager: Emmet Campos

Mexico–Texas Exchange Commission (M-TEC)

In a 1985 Memorandum of Understanding, the Texas Department of Agriculture and the Mexican Secretaría de Agricultura y Recursos Hidráulicos (agriculture and water resources) established the Mexico–Texas Exchange Commission. Not only has M-TEC facilitated an exchange of commercial and technical information on livestock, forestry, and agricultural production, but it has also increased trade between Texas and Mexico—especially those Mexican states bordering Texas. Texas is the only state to have a bilateral trade agreement with Mexico. For further information, contact Saúl Mercado.

Mexico–Texas Exchange Commission
Texas Department of Agriculture
P.O. Box 12847
Austin, Texas 78711
(512) 463-7624

State of Texas Office in Mexico

In 1987, this office published *Texas–Mexico: A Working Manual of Information, Procedures, Supports, and Guidelines on Trade between Texas and Mexico,* which includes useful listings of public- and private-sector agencies concerned with trade issues.

State of Texas Office in Mexico
Paseo de la Reforma 199, 7º piso
06500 México, D.F.
Tel. 566-3532 or 566-3350
Director: Felipe Mondragón

Mexico

Each of the six Mexican border states maintains an active interest in the border region, often through the state's secretariat of commerce and industrial development, and through its department of tourism. The state of Nuevo León maintains a commission for the development of northern Nuevo León (CODENOR). For details on these arrangements, contact the governor's office of each state.

6.4 STATE LEGISLATORS FROM U.S. BORDER STATES

The information for this section was obtained from the secretary of state's office in each state, and other sources where noted. Only representatives and senators whose districts adjoin the border are included.

Note: This information (concerning both officeholders and districts) will change after the November 1992 elections, which will reflect the redistricting currently under way. Also, the names in parentheses following the district numbers identify border counties included in a district. They do not necessarily include all counties making up that district, nor is all of the county necessarily included in the district.

Arizona

Arizona state senators and representatives may be contacted at: State Capitol / Phoenix, Arizona 85007 / (602) 542-4900.

SENATE

DISTRICT 5
(Yuma)

Jim Buster
4343 Fourteenth Lane
Yuma, Arizona 85364

DISTRICT 6
(Pima)

Alan Stephens
8050 South Fourteenth Street
Phoenix, Arizona 85040

DISTRICT 7
(Pima, Santa Cruz)

Peter D. Ríos
P.O. Box 451
Hayden, Arizona 85235

DISTRICT 8
(Cochise)

Gus Arzberger
Route 3, Box 6990
Wilcox, Arizona 85643

DISTRICT 9
(Santa Cruz)

John Dougherty
61 West Cedro Drive
Green Valley, Arizona 85614

HOUSE OF REPRESENTATIVES

DISTRICT 5
(Yuma)

Herb Guenther
P.O. Box 365
Tacna, Arizona 85352

Robert J. McLendon
777 Fourteenth Street
Yuma, Arizona 85364

DISTRICT 6
(Pima)

Henry Evans
1700 West Washington
Phoenix, Arizona 85007

Jim Hartdegen
11515 North Fantail Trail
Casa Grande, Arizona 85222

DISTRICT 7
(Pima, Santa Cruz)

Frank Celaya
P.O. Box 515
Florence, Arizona 85232

Richard Pacheco
P.O. Box 22348
Tucson, Arizona 85734

DISTRICT 8
(Cochise)

Rubén F. Ortega
500 Fry Blvd.
Sierra Vista, Arizona 85635

Mike Palmer
110 Mountain View
Bisbee, Arizona 85603

DISTRICT 9
(Santa Cruz)

Keith A. Bee
11171 East Escalante
Tucson, Arizona 85730

Marion L. Pickens
8743 East Twenty-ninth Street
Tucson, Arizona 85710

California

Information was provided by the reference department of the California State Library. Local addresses are listed below. Senators and assembly persons may also be contacted at: State Capitol / Sacramento, California 95814 / (916) 322-9900.

SENATE

DISTRICT 37
(Imperial)

Marian Bergeson
1101 Airport Road, suite C
Imperial, California 92251
(619) 353-8244

DISTRICT 39
(San Diego)

Lucy Killea
2550 Fifth Avenue, no. 152
San Diego, California 92103-6691
(619) 696-6955

DISTRICT 40
(San Diego)

Wadie Deddeh
368 Surrey Drive
Bonita, California 92002
(619) 427-7080

ASSEMBLY

DISTRICT 75
(San Diego)

Dede Alpert
3368 Governor Drive, suite C
San Diego, California 92122
(619) 457-5775

DISTRICT 80
(San Diego, Imperial)

Steve Peace
430 Davidson Street, suite B
Chula Vista, California 92010
(619) 426-1617

New Mexico

Information on New Mexico was compiled from the *State of New Mexico Roster,* available from: Secretary of State / Santa Fe, New Mexico 85703 / (505) 827-3600. The *Roster* also lists all county officials. New Mexico state senators and representatives may be contacted at: State Capitol Mailroom / Santa Fe, New Mexico 85703 / (505) 984-9300.

SENATE

DISTRICT 35
(Luna, Hidalgo)

John Arthur Smith
1202 Allen Street
Deming, New Mexico 88030
(505) 546-4979

DISTRICT 36
(Doña Ana)

Mary Jane García
P.O. Box 22
Doña Ana, New Mexico 88032
(505) 523-0440

DISTRICT 37
(Doña Ana)

Harold C. Foreman
2245 Thomas Drive
Las Cruces, New Mexico 88001
(505) 522-1068

DISTRICT 38
(Doña Ana)

Fernando R. Macías
701 West Parker
Las Cruces, New Mexico 88005
(505) 524-7809

HOUSE OF REPRESENTATIVES

DISTRICT 32
(Doña Ana, Luna)

G. X. McSherry
Route 2, Box 138
Deming, New Mexico 88030
(505) 546-8086

DISTRICT 33
(Doña Ana)

J. Paul Taylor
P.O. Box 133
Mesilla, New Mexico 88046
(505) 526-8949

DISTRICT 34
(Doña Ana)

David Martínez
179 Edgewood
Sunland Park, New Mexico 88063
(505) 589-7565

DISTRICT 35
(Doña Ana)

Ruben A. Smith
606 West Las Cruces Avenue
Las Cruces, New Mexico 88004
(505) 523-5517

DISTRICT 36
(Doña Ana)

William E. Porter
5200 North Highway 85
Las Cruces, New Mexico 88005
(505) 526-9335

DISTRICT 38
(Grant, Luna)

Murray Ryan
P.O. Box 110
Silver City, New Mexico 88062
(505) 538-2085

DISTRICT 37
(Doña Ana)

Leonard Lee Rawson
1681 Alta Vista Place
Las Cruces, New Mexico 88001
(505) 524-3568

DISTRICT 39
(Grant, Hidalgo)

Thomas P. Foy
2 Kilian Drive
Bayard, New Mexico 88023
(505) 538-2967

Texas

Texas senators and representatives may be contacted at: State Capitol Building / Austin, Texas 78701 / (512) 463-4630. Telephone numbers are listed for both Austin and district offices.

SENATE

DISTRICT 21
(Starr, Zapata, Webb, Maverick, Kinney)

Judith Zaffirini
P.O. Box 627
Laredo, Texas 78042
(512) 722-2293 (Laredo)
(512) 463-0121 (Austin)

DISTRICT 25
(Val Verde, Terrell, Brewster, Presidio, Jeff Davis, Hudspeth)

Bill Sims
P.O. Box 410
San Angelo, Texas 76902
(915) 658-5852 (San Angelo)
(512) 463-0125 (Austin)

DISTRICT 27
(Cameron, Hidalgo)

Eddie Lucio
P.O. Box 5958
Brownsville, Texas 78520
(512) 544-4644 (Brownsville)
(512) 463-0127 (Austin)

DISTRICT 29
(El Paso)

Peggy Rosson
1551 Montana Avenue, suite 201
El Paso, Texas 79902
(915) 544-1990 (El Paso)
(512) 463-0129 (Austin)

HOUSE OF REPRESENTATIVES

DISTRICT 37
(Starr)

Irma Rangel
318 North Seventh Street
Kingsville, Texas 78363
(512) 592-5142 (Kingsville)
(512) 463-0666 (Austin)

DISTRICT 40
(Hidalgo)

Eddie de la Garza
222 West Cano
Edinburg, Texas 78539
(512) 383-1424 (Edinburg)
(512) 463-0636 (Austin)

DISTRICT 38
(Cameron)

Ken Fleuriet
510 East Harrison
Harlingen, Texas 78550
(512) 421-2760 (Harlingen)
(512) 463-0606 (Austin)

DISTRICT 41
(Hidalgo)

Roberto Gutiérrez
2425 Griffin Parkway, suite 101
Mission, Texas 78572
(512) 581-3441 (Mission)
(512) 463-0578 (Austin)

DISTRICT 39
(Cameron)

René Oliveira
422 East Elizabeth
Brownsville, Texas 78520
(512) 544-2764 (Brownsville)
(512) 463-0640 (Austin)

DISTRICT 42
(Hidalgo)

Renato Cuéllar
115 East Fifth Street, suite 2
Weslaco, Texas 78596
(512) 968-2648 (Weslaco)
(512) 463-0530 (Austin)

DISTRICT 43
(Webb)

Henry Cuéllar
P.O. Box 757
Laredo, Texas 78042
(512) 725-8988 (Laredo)
(512) 463-0558 (Austin)

DISTRICT 44
(Zapata)

Ernestine Glossbrenner
P.O. Drawer 2188
Alice, Texas 78333
(512) 664-5868 (Alice)
(512) 463-0544 (Austin)

DISTRICT 68
(Maverick, Kinney, Val Verde,
Terrell, Brewster, Presidio)

Pete Gallego
P.O. Box 777
Alpine, Texas 79831
(915) 840-1543 (Alpine)
(512) 463-0566 (Austin)

DISTRICT 69
(Jeff Davis, Hudspeth)

Troy Frasier
208 West Third
Big Spring, Texas 79720
(915) 263-1307 (Big Spring)
(512) 463-0688 (Austin)

DISTRICT 70
(El Paso)

Jack Vowell
4849 North Mesa Street, suite 312-A
El Paso, Texas 79912
(915) 542-1936 (El Paso)
(512) 463-0728 (Austin)

DISTRICT 71
(El Paso)

Pat Haggerty
2267 Trawood, no. B-5
El Paso, Texas 79935
(915) 591-4471 (El Paso)
(512) 463-0596 (Austin)

DISTRICT 72
(El Paso)

Paul Moreno
2314 Montana Avenue
El Paso, Texas 79903
(915) 544-0789 (El Paso)
(512) 463-0638 (Austin)

DISTRICT 73
(El Paso)

Nancy McDonald
7500 Viscount, suite 116
El Paso, Texas 79925
(915) 778-5477 (El Paso)
(512) 463-0622 (Austin)

DISTRICT 74
(El Paso)

Nicolás Pérez
1515 Montana Avenue
El Paso, Texas 79907
(915) 532-6914 (El Paso)
(512) 463-0654 (Austin)

7 MAQUILADORA-RELATED ORGANIZATIONS

7.1 OVERVIEW

The Border Industrialization Program, also referred to as the in-bond, twin-plant, or *maquiladora* program, was initiated by the Mexican government in 1965, and allows foreign companies to operate assembly and manufacturing plants in Mexico. Although it is not possible to give precise figures due to the fluctuating nature of *maquiladora* operations, it is safe to say that at the beginning of 1991 there were over 1,800 such plants, employing 430,000 workers. Approximately three-quarters of the plants were located in five border cities: Tijuana, Mexicali, Nogales, Ciudad Juárez, and Matamoros. Tijuana had the largest number of plants, while Ciudad Juárez plants all together employed the largest number of workers.

A useful source of information on the *maquiladoras* is Sklair's *Maquiladoras: An Annotated Bibiliography and Research Guide to Mexico's In-Bond Industry*. Also helpful is Clement's *Maquiladora Resource Guide: Exploring the Maquiladora/In-Bond Option in Baja California, Mexico*, published by San Diego State University. A listing of all plants, industrial parks, promoters, and *maquiladora* associations is available in the *Directory of In-Bond Plants (Maquiladoras) in Mexico*, published annually by Mexico Communications. Additional information is provided in AMCHAM's *Mexico's Maquiladora In-Bond Industry Handbook*, and SANDAG's *The Bridge: Baja California Regional Industrial Development Guide*. (*See Chapter 10 for complete bibliographic references for these works, and for a listing of periodicals that focus on* maquiladoras.)

The listings below include groups that promote the *maquiladora* program. In addition, local chambers of commerce can provide information about *maquiladora* operations in their communities.

7.2 NATIONAL AND REGIONAL ORGANIZATIONS

AMERICAN CHAMBER OF COMMERCE OF MEXICO, A.C.

The chamber publishes a monthly, *The Maquiladora Newsletter,* which provides up-to-date information on the *maquiladora* program.

American Chamber of Commerce of Mexico, A.C.
Lucerna 78
06600 México, D.F.
Tel. 705-0995

BORDER TRADE ALLIANCE (BTA)

Composed of border-area economic development corporations, chambers of commerce, trade associations, banks, industrial parks, service providers, manufacturers, and state and local government agencies, the Border Trade Alliance is a network founded in 1986 to act as a forum for its members to discuss and promote their interests. Although the BTA's agenda includes transportation, health, and environmental issues, its primary concern has been with the in-bond industries. The BTA has quickly grown to be a very important advocate for the *maquiladora* program.

Border Trade Alliance
c/o San Diego Economic Development Corporation
701 B Street, suite 1850
San Diego, California 92101
(619) 234-8484

COMMITTEE FOR PRODUCTION SHARING

Formerly known as the Committee for 806.30 and 807, Inc., this group lobbies to protect U.S. companies operating under items 806.30 and 807 of the U.S. Tariff Code.

Committee for Production Sharing
1629 K Street, suite 801
Washington, D.C. 20006
(202) 296-3232

Secretaría de Comercio y Fomento Industrial (SECOFI)
(*secretariat of commerce and industrial development*)

A department of the Mexican federal government, SECOFI approves applications for establishing *maquiladoras*. Listings for SECOFI offices along the border can be found in Chapter 4, section 2.

Subdirección de la Industria Maquiladora y Desarrollo Regional
(*suboffice of the maquiladora industry and regional development*)

Subdirección de la Industria Maquiladora y Desarrollo Regional
Periférico Sur 3025
Colonia Héroes de Padierna
10700 México, D.F.
Tel. 683-3918 or 683-4394

7.3 LOCAL BORDER DEVELOPMENT ORGANIZATIONS

These organizations, most of which are almost exclusively concerned with the promotion of *maquiladoras,* can provide locations of and other information on industrial parks in Mexico. (For a detailed listing of *maquiladora* operations on the border, see Mexico Communication's *Directory of In-Bond Plants (Maquiladoras) in Mexico,* listed in Chapter 10, section 1.)

Mexico

Baja California

CALEXICO

Comisión de Desarrollo Industrial
de Mexicali
Justo Sierra y Larroque, despacho 1
21000 Mexicali, Baja California
Tel. 52-6780
•*U.S. mailing address:*
 P.O. Box 6343
 Calexico, California 92231

TIJUANA

Asociación de la Industria
 Maquiladora
Zona Costa de Baja California, A.C.
Apartado Postal 428
22000 Tijuana, Baja California
Tel. 81-6438

Comisión de Fomento Industrial
 y de Comercio Internacional de
 Tijuana-Tecate
Apartado Postal 1798
22000 Tijuana, Baja California
Tel. 81-7716
•*U.S. mailing address:*
 P.O. Box 2985
 San Ysidro, California 92073

Chihuahua

CIUDAD JUÁREZ

Asociación de Maquiladoras de
  Ciudad Juárez, A.C.
Río Nilo 4049-9-B
32310 Ciudad Juárez, Chihuahua
Tel. 13-4257

Desarrollo Económico de Ciudad
  Juárez, A.C.
Adolfo de la Huerta 742-3
32340 Ciudad Juárez, Chihuahua
Tel. 16-3268

Maquiladora Association
Apartado Postal 600
34257 Ciudad Juárez, Chihuahua
Tel. 16-1461

Promotora de la Industria
  Chihuahuense
Apartado Postal 1621
32340 Ciudad Juárez, Chihuahua
Tel. 16-5752

Coahuila

CIUDAD ACUÑA

Asociación de Maquiladoras de Ciudad Acuña/Del Rio, A.C.
•U.S. mailing address:
P.O. Box 420211
Del Rio, Texas 78842

Sonora

NOGALES

Asociación de Maquiladoras de
  México, A.C.
Apartado Postal 495
84000 Nogales, Sonora
•U.S. mailing address:
P.O. Box 893
Nogales, Arizona 85629

SAN LUIS RÍO COLORADO

Operadores del Parque Industrial
•U.S. mailing address & tel.:
P.O. Box 3077
San Luis, Arizona 85349
(602) 534-2534

93

Tamaulipas

Secretaría de Fomento Comercial, Industrial y Turístico
Gobierno Estatal de Tamaulipas
Torre Gubernamental J.L.P., 10º piso
87000 Ciudad Victoria, Tamaulipas
Tel. 2-5551

United States

Arizona

DOUGLAS

Douglas Chamber of Commerce
P.O. Drawer F
Douglas, Arizona 85608
(602) 364-2477

NOGALES

Border Industrial Development
  Corporation
P.O. Box 1688
Kino Park
Nogales, Arizona 85628
(602) 287-3685

SAN LUIS

Town of San Luis
Economic Development
  Corporation
P.O. Box S
San Luis, Arizona 85349
(602) 627-8143

YUMA

Yuma County Development
  Authority
P.O. Box 320
Yuma, Arizona 85364
(602) 783-0193

Yuma Economic Development
  Corporation
P.O. Box 230
Yuma, Arizona 85364
(602) 783-0193

California

CHULA VISTA

Western Maquiladora Trade
  Association
P.O. Box 3927
Chula Vista, California 92011
(619) 435-5369

SAN DIEGO

San Diego Economic Development
  Corporation
701 B Street, suite 1850
San Diego, California 92101
(619) 234-8484

EL CENTRO

Regional Economic Development,
  Inc.
1411 State Street
El Centro, California 92244
(619) 353-5050

New Mexico

DEMING

Luna County Economic Development Corporation
109 East Pine
Deming, New Mexico 88030
(505) 546-8848

Texas

BROWNSVILLE

Industrial Development
Brownsville Chamber of
  Commerce
P.O. Box 752
Brownsville, Texas 78520
(512) 542-4341

CARRIZO SPRINGS

Middle Rio Grande Development
  Council
P.O. Box 702
Carrizo Springs, Texas 78834
(512) 876-3533

DEL RIO

Del Rio Chamber of Commerce
1915 Avenue F
Del Rio, Texas 78834
(512) 775-3551

EAGLE PASS

Eagle Pass Chamber of Commerce
P.O. Box 1188
Eagle Pass, Texas 78853
(512) 773-3224

Maverick County Office of
  Economic Development
P.O. Box 955
Eagle Pass, Texas 78853
(512) 773-4110

EL PASO

El Paso Economic Development
  Department
7 Civic Center Plaza
El Paso, Texas 79901
(915) 533-4284

El Paso Industrial Development
  Corporation
9 Civic Center Plaza
El Paso, Texas 79901
(915) 532-8281

Maquila Information Exchange
  Network
4120 Rio Bravo, suite 204
El Paso, Texas 79902
(915) 542-1056

HARLINGEN

Harlingen Area Chamber of
  Commerce
P.O. Box 189
Harlingen, Texas 78551
(512) 423-5440

LAREDO

Laredo Development Foundation
P.O. Box 1435
Laredo, Texas 78042
(512) 722-0563

MCALLEN

McAllen Industrial Board
10 North Broadway
McAllen, Texas 78502
(512) 682-2875

PHARR

Pharr Industrial Foundation
P.O. Box 59
Pharr, Texas 78577
(512) 781-1676

RIO GRANDE CITY

Starr County Industrial Foundation
P.O. Box 502
Rio Grande City, Texas 78582
(512) 487-2709

WESLACO

Rio Grande Valley Industrial
  Commission
P.O. Box 975
Weslaco, Texas 78596
(512) 968-3141

7.4 CANACINTRA

CANACINTRA, the Cámara Nacional de la Industria de Transformación (*national chamber of industry of transformation*), is involved in promoting industrial development. CANACINTRA often works with the Banco Nacional de México (BANAMEX) to finance ventures it is promoting. Within the structure of CANACINTRA is the Asociación de Maquiladoras de México, which represents the interests of the *maquiladoras* in Mexico. All Mexican manufacturing firms are required to belong to CANACINTRA. Its offices in Mexico City and in border communities are listed below.

CANACINTRA
Avenida San Antonio 256
03810 México, D.F.
Tel. 563-3400

Baja California

CANACINTRA
Calzada Justo Sierra y J. María
  Larroque
Colonia Nueva
21100 Mexicali, Baja California
Tel. 52-9810

CANACINTRA
Bulevar Gustavo Díaz Ordaz y
  Bugambilias
Fraccionamiento El Prado
22440 Tijuana, Baja California
Tel. 81-6644

Chihuahua

CANACINTRA
Centro Comerical PRONAF, locales 45 y 47
32310 Ciudad Juárez, Chihuahua
Tel. 6-3457

Coahuila

CANACINTRA
Calle Periodistas 701, 1er piso
Colonia Burócrata
26020 Piedras Negras, Coahuila
Tel. 2-1421

Sonora

CANACINTRA
Bulevar Benito Juárez, Oeste
83600 Caborca, Sonora
Tel. 2-1337

CANACINTRA
Avenida Obregón 1010-2
Edificio MAS, centro
84000 Nogales, Sonora
Tel. 2-4750

CANACINTRA
Avenida Obregón entre 14 y 15
Edificio Canaco, altos, centro
83400 San Luis Río Colorado,
  Sonora
Tel. 4-2147

Tamaulipas

CANACINTRA
Calle Herrera 6, 2º piso, centro
87300 Matamoros, Tamaulipas
Tel. 2-1327

CANACINTRA
Avenida Guerrero 810, centro
88000 Nuevo Laredo, Tamaulipas
Tel. 2-5888

CANACINTRA
Calle Matías Canales 603
Colonia Ribereña
88620 Reynosa, Tamaulipas
Tel. 3-6259

CANACINTRA
Niños Héroes y Saltillo s/n, centro
88900 Río Bravo, Tamaulipas
Tel. 4-3711

8 COMMUNICATIONS MEDIA

8.1 NEWSPAPERS

The following listing includes newspapers published in both Mexican and U.S. border communities. Although the entries for U.S. newspapers are thought to be complete, we were not able to obtain a comprehensive listing of Mexican newspapers. We did include, however, several nonborder newspapers that receive wide circulation in border communities. Many of the major Mexico City dailies are also available in the larger Mexican border cities, but these are not listed. Information for this section was drawn primarily from the *1989 Media Encyclopedia: The Working Press of the Nation, Volume I—Newspaper Directory* (Chicago: National Research Bureau, 1988); *Editor and Publisher International Yearbook* (New York: Editor and Publisher, 1987); and *Medios impresos* (México, D.F.: Medios Publicatarios Mexicanos, 1988).

United States

Arizona

BISBEE

Bisbee Daily Review
12 Main Street
Bisbee, Arizona 85603
(602) 432-2231

DOUGLAS

Douglas Dispatch
530 Eleventh Street
Douglas, Arizona 85608
(602) 364-3424

NOGALES

Nogales Daily Herald
134 Grand Avenue
Nogales, Arizona 85621
(602) 287-3622

Nogales International
977 Grand Avenue
Nogales, Arizona 85621
(602) 287-9444

SIERRA VISTA

Sierra Vista Herald
102 Fab Street
Sierra Vista, Arizona 85635
(602) 458-9440

TUCSON

Arizona Daily Star
P.O. Box 26807
Tucson, Arizona 85726
(602) 573-4400

Tucson Citizen
4850 South Park
Tucson, Arizona 85726
(602) 294-4433

YUMA

Yuma Daily Sun
P.O. Box 271
Yuma, Arizona 85364
(602) 783-3333

California

CALEXICO

Calexico Chronicle
305 Rockwood Avenue
Calexico, California 92231
(619) 357-3214

IMPERIAL VALLEY

Imperial Valley Press
P.O. Box 2770
El Centro, California 92244
(619) 352-2211

LOS ANGELES

Los Angeles Times
Times Mirror Square
Los Angeles, California 90053
(213) 237-5000

La Opinión de Los Angeles
1436 South Main Street
Los Angeles, California 90015
(213) 748-1191

SAN DIEGO

La Prensa de San Diego [weekly]
1950 Fifth Avenue, suites 1–3
San Diego, California 92101
(619) 231-2873

San Diego Evening Tribune
P.O. Box 191
San Diego, California 92112
(619) 299-3131

San Diego Union
P.O. Box 191
San Diego, California 92112
(619) 299-3131

El Sol de San Diego [weekly]
1879 Logan Avenue, suite M
San Diego, California 92113
(619) 233-8496

New Mexico

ALBUQUERQUE

Albuquerque Journal
P.O. Drawer J
Albuquerque, New Mexico 87103
(505) 823-7777

Albuquerque Tribune
P.O. Drawer T
Albuquerque, New Mexico 87103
(505) 823-7777

DEMING

Deming Headlight
P.O. Box 881
Deming, New Mexico 88031
(505) 546-2611

LAS CRUCES

Las Cruces Sun-News
P.O. Box 1749
Las Cruces, New Mexico 88004
(505) 523-4581

Texas

ALPINE

Alpine Avalanche [weekly]
P.O. Box 719
Alpine, Texas 79830
(915) 837-3334

DEL RIO

Del Rio News-Herald
321 South Main Street
Del Rio, Texas 78840
(512) 775-1551

EAGLE PASS

Eagle Pass News-Guide [biweekly]
P.O. Box 764
Eagle Pass, Texas 78853
(512) 773-2309

EL PASO

El Paso Herald Post
P.O. Box 20
El Paso, Texas 79999
(915) 546-6365

El Paso Times
P.O. Box 20
El Paso, Texas 79999
(915) 546-6100

LAREDO

Laredo Morning Times
P.O. Box 2127
Laredo, Texas 78041
(512) 723-2901

Laredo News
P.O. Box 1928
Laredo, Texas 78040
(512) 724-8386

LOWER RIO GRANDE VALLEY

Brownsville Herald
1135 East Van Buren
Brownsville, Texas 78520
(512) 542-4301

Brownsville Times [biweekly]
P.O. Box 472
Brownsville, Texas 78520
(512) 542-3504

Edinburg Daily Review
215 East University Avenue
Edinburg, Texas 78539
(512) 383-2705

Harlingen Valley Morning Star
P.O. Box 511
Harlingen, Texas 78551
(512) 423-5511

Mercedes Enterprise [weekly]
P.O. Box 657
Mercedes, Texas 78570
(512) 565-2425

McAllen Monitor
1100 Ash Street
McAllen, Texas 78501
(512) 686-4343

Pharr Advance News [weekly]
1101 North Cage
Pharr, Texas 78577
(512) 783-0371

Port Isabel–South Padre Press
[biweekly]
P.O. Box 308
Port Isabel, Texas 78578
(512) 943-5545

San Benito News [weekly]
P.O. Drawer 1791
San Benito, Texas 78586
(512) 399-2436

Weslaco Mid-Valley News
[biweekly]
P.O. Box 207
Weslaco, Texas 78596
(512) 968-3139

SAN ANTONIO

San Antonio Express News
P.O. Box 2171
San Antonio, Texas 78297
(512) 225-7411

San Antonio Light
P.O. Box 161
San Antonio, Texas 78291
(512) 271-2700

Mexico

Baja California

El Centinela
Avenida Madero 1545
Mexicali, Baja California
Tel. 52-9580

Novedades de Baja California
Avenida de la Patria 952
Mexicali, Baja California
Tel. 57-4801

La Voz de la Frontera
Avenida Madero 1545
Mexicali, Baja California
Tel. 53-4545

ABC
Bulevar Agua Caliente 2700,
  esquina Avenida Jalisco
Tijuana, Baja California
Tel. 84-1644

El Heraldo de Baja California
Río Colorado 315
Tijuana, Baja California
Tel. 86-4314

El Mexicano
Carretera al Aeropuerto s/n
Tijuana, Baja California
Tel. 86-8001

Periódico Baja California
Bulevar Agua Caliente 4358,
  7º piso
Tijuana, Baja California
Tel. 81-7222

Ultimas Noticias
Carretera al Aeropuerto s/n
Tijuana, Baja California
Tel. 86-8001

Zeta
Avenida de las Américas 25-A
Fraccionamiento El Paraíso
Tijuana, Baja California
Tel. 81-4156

Chihuahua

CIUDAD JUÁREZ

El Diario de Juárez
Paseo Triunfo de la República y
  Anillo Envolvente de PRONAF
Ciudad Juárez, Chihuahua
Tel. 16-0006

El Fronterizo
Ramón Corona y Galeana
Ciudad Juárez, Chihuahua
Tel. 12-1980

El Mexicano
Ramón Corona y Galeana
Ciudad Juárez, Chihuahua
Tel. 12-1980

El Universal de Ciudad Juárez
Avenida Valle de Juárez 6689
Ciudad Juárez, Chihuahua
Tel. 17-0044

Coahuila

CIUDAD ACUÑA

El Coahuilense
2 de Abril 755
Ciudad Acuña, Coahuila

El Zócalo
Bravo y Emiliano Zapata
Ciudad Acuña, Coahuila
Tel. 2-0405

PIEDRAS NEGRAS

El Diario
Piedras Negras, Coahuila
Tel. 2-0910
•*U.S. mailing address:*
 P.O. Box 375
 Eagle Pass, Texas 78853

La Voz del Norte
E. Carranza 1300
Piedras Negras, Coahuila

El Zócalo
Avenida Cuautémoc 714
Piedras Negras, Coahuila

Nuevo León

El Norte
Washington Oriente 629
Apartado Postal 186
Monterrey, Nuevo León
Tel. 45-5100

Sonora

HERMOSILLO

El Imparcial
Apartado Postal 66
Hermosillo, Sonora
Tel. 2-2900

El Sonorense
Bulevar Transversal y Royal
Hermosillo, Sonora
Tel. 3-3205

NOGALES

El Diario de Nogales
Avenida Obregón 1199, altos
Nogales, Sonora

La Voz del Norte
Apartado Postal 776
Nogales, Sonora
Tel. 2-7171

SAN LUIS RÍO COLORADO

El Heraldo
Callejón Obregón y Cinco A
San Luis Río Colorado, Sonora

Tribuna de San Luis
Calle Sexta y Avenida Juárez,
no. 325
San Luis Río Colorado, Sonora
Tel. 4-2542

Tamaulipas

MATAMOROS

El Bravo
Morelos y Primera, no. 129
Matamoros, Tamaulipas
Tel. 2-4700

La Opinión
Lauro Villar 200
Matamoros, Tamaulipas
Tel. 3-7757

La Prensa de Matamoros
Guerrero 71-A
Matamoros, Tamaulipas

Y Punto
Avenida de las Americas 1
Matamoros, Tamaulipas
Tel. 2-4211

NUEVO LAREDO

El Correo
González 2409
Nuevo Laredo, Tamaulipas
Tel. 2-8444

El Diario
González 2409
Nuevo Laredo, Tamaulipas
Tel. 2-8444

El Manaña
Juárez y Perú
Nuevo Laredo, Tamaulipas
Tel. 4-8219

La Prensa de Nuevo Laredo
González 2409
Nuevo Laredo, Tamaulipas

REYNOSA

El Manaña
Apartado Postal 14
Reynosa, Tamaulipas
Tel. 3-6415

La Prensa de Reynosa
González Ortega y Matamoros
Reynosa, Tamaulipas
Tel. 2-3515

La Tarde
Apartado Postal 14
Reynosa, Tamaulipas
Tel. 3-6662

8.2 RADIO STATIONS

Because it is impossible to obtain an accurate, comprehensive listing of radio stations, and because the turnover rate in call letters is so high, radio listings are not included in this guide. Partial listings for the United States are available in *Broadcasting Cable Yearbook* (Washington, D.C.: Broadcasting Publications, annual). For radio listings in Mexican border cities, see Norma Iglesias, *Panorama de los medios de comunicación en la frontera norte* (Tijuana: Fundación Manuel Buendía, and Programa Cultural de las Fronteras, Colegio de la Frontera Norte, 1989). Local telephone directories are the best source for the most current information.

8.3   TELEVISION STATIONS

The listings below include only those stations located in border communities. Of course, due to the rapid expansion of cable services and satellite relay stations, many other channels are received along the border as well.

United States

Arizona

YUMA

KYEL
1301 South Third Avenue
Yuma, Arizona 85364
(602) 782-5113

California

IMPERIAL VALLEY

KECY
778 State
El Centro, California 92243
(619) 353-9990

SAN DIEGO

KCST-TV
P.O. Box 11039
San Diego, California 92111
(619) 279-3939

KFMB-TV
P.O. Box 80888
San Diego, California 92138
(619) 571-8888

KGTV-TV
P.O. Box 85347
San Diego, California 92138
(619) 237-1010

KPBS-TV
San Diego State University
San Diego, California 92182
(619) 265-6415

New Mexico

LAS CRUCES

KRWG-TV
New Mexico State University
Box TV 22
Las Cruces, New Mexico 88003
(505) 646-2222

Texas

EL PASO

KCIK-TV
3100 North Stanton
El Paso, Texas 79902
(915) 533-1414

KCOS-TV
University of Texas at El Paso
El Paso, Texas 79968
(915) 532-6013

KDBC-TV
2201 Wyoming
El Paso, Texas 79903
(915) 532-6551

KINT-TV
5426 North Mesa Street
El Paso, Texas 79912
(915) 880-2626

KTSM-TV
801 North Oregon Street
El Paso, Texas 79902
(915) 532-5421

KVIA-TV
4140 Rio Bravo
El Paso, Texas 79902
(915) 532-7777

LAREDO

KGNS-TV
102 West Del Mar Blvd.
Laredo, Texas 78041
(512) 727-8888

KVTV-TV
P.O. Box 2039
Laredo, Texas 78041
(512) 723-2923

LOWER RIO GRANDE VALLEY

KGBT-TV
1519 West Harrison
Harlingen, Texas 78551
(512) 421-4444

KMBH-TV
1701 East Tennessee Street
Harlingen, Texas 78551
(512) 421-4111

KRGV-TV
900 East Expressway
Weslaco, Texas 78596
(512) 968-5555

Mexico

Baja California

MEXICALI

XHAQ-TV
Calle Mina 200
Mexicali, Baja California

XHBC-TV
Madero 714
Mexicali, Baja California

TIJUANA

XEWT-TV
Apartado Postal 12
Tijuana, Baja California
Tel. 84-5185

XHAS-TV
Plaza Vendome
Bulevar Agua Caliente 802-J
Tijuana, Baja California
Tel. 86-4136

Chihuahua

CIUDAD JUÁREZ

XEJ-TV
Avenida Vicente Guerrero
  Oriente 732
Ciudad Juárez, Chihuahua
Tel. 15-1585

XHIJ-TV
Avenida Vicente Guerrero
  Oriente 2526
Ciudad Juárez, Chihuahua
Tel. 14-4444

Tamaulipas

MATAMOROS

XRIO-TV
•*U.S. mailing address & tel.:*
500 East Beaumont
McAllen, Texas 78501
(512) 687-5206

NUEVO LAREDO

XEFE-TV
Los Fresnos, kilómetro 5
Nuevo Laredo, Tamaulipas
Tel. 4-6857

9 EDUCATIONAL RESOURCES

Asociación Nacional de Universidades e Institutos de Enseñanza Superior (ANUIES)
(*national association of universities and institutes of higher education*)

Formed in 1950, ANUIES is composed of seventy-eight institutions that represent nearly all of Mexico's public institutions and several of its private institutions. The goals of ANUIES include: studying the academic, administrative, and economic problems of higher education in Mexico; promoting exchanges of personnel, information, and services between member institutions; and representing its member institutions both within and outside of Mexico. ANUIES is the Mexican counterpart of PROFMEX (*see below*).

Asociación Nacional de Universidades e Institutos
  de Enseñanza Superior
Avenida Insurgentes Sur 2133, 3ᵉʳ piso
01000 México, D.F.
Tel. 550-2755

Association of Borderlands Scholars

Founded in 1976 to promote the study of the U.S.–Mexico border region, this association is international and interdisciplinary, with members representing a wide variety of academic and professional areas. Publications of the ABS include the biannual *Journal of Borderlands Studies* and a newsletter, *La Frontera*. Annual meetings of the association are held in conjunction with the Western Social Science Association each spring. Annual membership dues are $25 and include a subscription to both publications, as well as a membership directory listing addresses and phone numbers of the association's 144 members.

Association of Borderlands Scholars
Department of Economics
Box 30001, Dept. 3CQ
New Mexico State University
Las Cruces, New Mexico 88003
(505) 646-2113

PROFMEX

PROFMEX, the Consortium of U.S. Research Programs for Mexico, was established to facilitate communication among individuals and institutions having common interests in Mexico and the U.S.–Mexican relationship. PROFMEX coordinates U.S. academic programs focusing on Mexico and promotes scholarly exchanges with Mexican colleagues and institutions. Membership is open to academic institutions, educational and nonprofit organizations, private corporations, and individuals.

PROFMEX sponsors an annual symposium in conjunction with its Mexican counterpart, ANUIES (*see above*).

George Baker, Executive Secretary
PROFMEX
1440 Euclid Avenue
Berkeley, California 94708
(415) 486-1247

PROFMEX PUBLICATIONS

MEXICO POLICY NEWS

Published twice yearly, this newsletter covers contemporary policy issues.

Paul Ganster, Editor
Mexico Policy News
San Diego State University
San Diego, California 92182
(619) 594-5423

PROFMEX LETTER

This letter provides a forum for members' writings-in-progress.

George Baker, Executive Secretary
(*see above*)

PROFMEX MONOGRAPH SERIES

Published by the University of Arizona on behalf of PROFMEX, this is a special series of scholarly studies and reports.

Michael Meyer, Editor
PROFMEX Monograph Series
Department of History
University of Arizona
Tucson, Arizona 85721
(602) 621-1586

CONFERENCE PROCEEDINGS

These are published jointly with ANUIES. By 1989, four volumes had been published.

George Baker, Executive Secretary
(*see above*)

Inactive Organizations

BORDER COLLEGE CONSORTIUM

Established in 1969, the consortium was a loose association of seven border-region community colleges that shared ideas and resources, and discussed common problems. It was composed of Texas Southmost College (Brownsville, Texas), Laredo Junior College, El Paso Community College, Cochise College (Douglas, Arizona), Arizona Western College (Yuma, Arizona), Imperial Valley College (El Centro, California), and Southwestern College (Chula Vista, California). The consortium held workshops in association with their Mexican counterparts, which included the Regional Technical Institutes in Matamoros, Nuevo Laredo, Piedras Negras, Ciudad Juárez, Chihuahua, Nogales, Mexicali, and Tijuana. In early 1991 the consortium was inactive.

BORDER STATE UNIVERSITY CONSORTIUM FOR LATIN AMERICA (BSUCLA)

Composed of several border-area universities, from 1969 to 1983 BSUCLA worked to coordinate teaching and research on Latin America having a particular focus on the U.S.–Mexico border region. In 1983 BSUCLA was disbanded and its members incorporated into PROFMEX. BSUCLA records are archived at New Mexico State University in the library's Rio Grande Historical Collection.

ESTUDIOS REGIONALES MÉXICO–ESTADOS UNIDOS, A.C.
(*U.S.–Mexico regional studies*)

This organization was founded in 1983, but is currently inactive. Made up of Mexican research institutes and universities, it was dedicated to promoting the study of the impact of neighboring countries on regions within Mexico. It was particularly interested in the effect of the United States on the northern Mexican border region.

9.2 UNIVERSITIES, RESEARCH CENTERS, AND COLLEGES

United States

Arizona

ARIZONA STATE UNIVERSITY

CENTER FOR LATIN AMERICAN STUDIES

Established in 1967, this center has approximately seventy-five faculty affiliates engaged in research on a wide array of topics related to Mexico. Its activities include conferences, lecture series, film festivals, and a substantial community outreach program.

Center for Latin American Studies
Arizona State University
Tempe, Arizona 85281
(602) 965-5127
Interim Director: Teresa Valdivieso

HISPANIC RESEARCH CENTER

Established in 1985, the center is an interdisciplinary research unit focusing on entrepreneurship, science and technology, the Hispanic polity, and the arts. It has a very active publications program that includes the *Bilingual Review/Press.*

Hispanic Research Center
Arizona State University
Tempe, Arizona 85287
(602) 965-3990
Director: Raymond V. Padilla

University of Arizona

Bureau of Applied Research in Anthropology, Borderlands Section

The Borderlands Section of the bureau investigates problems of common interest to the United States and Mexico. These include the study of interethnic relations, rural and urban development, immigration and migration, international border relations, and cross-cultural adaptation and coping strategies.

Borderlands Section
Bureau of Applied Research in Anthropology
Department of Anthropology
University of Arizona
Tucson, Arizona 85721
(602) 621-6282
Section Head: James A. Greenberg

Documentary Relations of the Southwest (DRSW)

The DRSW is an interdisciplinary, multiphase project involving extensive archival research, the critical selection and annotation of primary documents, and bilingual publication of these documents, all pertaining to the history and cultural heritage of the southwestern United States and northern Mexico.

Documentary Relations of the Southwest
Arizona State Museum
University of Arizona
Tucson, Arizona 85721
(602) 621-6278
Director: Charles Polzer, S.J.

Latin America Area Center

The center sponsors conferences and speakers on borderlands topics. It published the first edition of the present book, then titled *The United States–Mexico Border: A Guide to Institutions, Organizations, and Scholars.*

124

Through the University of Arizona Press the center publishes a scholarly series for PROFMEX (*see "PROFMEX" in the first section of this chapter*).

Latin America Area Center
University of Arizona
Tucson, Arizona 85721
(602) 621-1137
Director: Donna Guy

Mexican American Studies and Research Center (MASRC)

The center sponsors research on Mexican American issues, and publishes *Perspectives in Mexican American Studies* and the *Renato Rosaldo Lecture Monograph Series.*

Mexican American Studies & Research Center
University of Arizona
Tucson, Arizona 85721
(602) 621-7551
Director: Macario Saldate IV

Rural Health Office

This office has been interested in border health issues for over fifteen years. It has a Border Working Group, and has established a close relationship with health projects in the adjacent Mexican state of Sonora.

Rural Health Office
Department of Family & Community Medicine
University of Arizona
Tucson, Arizona 85721
(602) 626-7946
Director: Andrew Nichols, M.D.

Southwest Center

Established in 1987, this center is dedicated to preserving the unique social and cultural history of the American Southwest and northwestern Mexico. Its goal is to encourage the exchange of ideas, research, publications, and public outreach by scholars at the University of Arizona and other educational institutions throughout the United States. The center publishes the *Journal of the Southwest* (formerly *Arizona and the West*), which includes studies on borderland topics.

Southwest Center
University of Arizona
Tucson, Arizona 85721
(602) 621-2484
Director: Joseph C. Wilder

Southwest Institute for Research on Women (SIROW)

SIROW conducts research on the experience of women in the Southwest, with emphasis on multicultural issues, educational issues, and the impact of regional growth on women (particularly elderly women).

Southwest Institute for Research on Women
University of Arizona
Tucson, Arizona 85721
(602) 621-7338
Executive Director: Janice Monk

Udall Center for Studies in Public Policy

The Udall Center has organized a university-wide Border Policy Group composed of researchers interested in such border topics as the *maquiladoras,* U.S. immigration policy, informal networks and delivery systems, and the social cost of border-area public policies. The center has also compiled a directory of borderlands scholars at the University of Arizona.

Udall Center for Studies in Public Policy
University of Arizona
Tucson, Arizona 85721
(602) 621-7189
Director: Helen Ingram

COLLEGES

Arizona Western College
Box 929
Yuma, Arizona 85364
(602) 726-1000

Cochise College
Douglas, Arizona 85607
(602) 364-7943

California

SAN DIEGO STATE UNIVERSITY

INSTITUTE FOR BORDER STUDIES (IBS)

This institute was created in 1983 in order to encourage and conduct research on border issues, and to serve as a border information center. Conferences sponsored by the IBS promote cooperation among border communities and allow for the exchange of information on specific border topics.

Institute for Border Studies
San Diego State University
Imperial Valley Campus
Calexico, California 92231
(619) 357-3193
Director: Reynaldo Ayala

INSTITUTE FOR REGIONAL STUDIES OF THE CALIFORNIAS

This institute was created in 1983 in response to the diversity of border- and Mexico-related activities at San Diego State University, and the need in the larger community for a more concerted approach to regional and transboundary problems and prospects. It has an active program of courses, conferences, seminars, and public lectures. Its publications include a Border Issues Series and a Border Studies Series.

Institute for Regional Studies of the Californias
San Diego State University
San Diego, California 92182
(619) 594-5423
Director: Paul Ganster

MEXICAN AMERICAN STUDIES DEPARTMENT

This department offers courses in U.S.–Mexico border relations, and a Border Certificate Program.

Mexican American Studies Department
San Diego State University
San Diego, California 92182
(619) 594-6452
Chair: Richard Griswold del Castillo

UNIVERSITY OF CALIFORNIA, IRVINE

PROGRAM IN COMPARATIVE CULTURE

This program explores contemporary conflicts and contrasts in the U.S.–Mexico border region, including the relationship between the goals of Mexico's national economic policy and the development of northern Mexican regions subject to U.S. economic influence.

Program in Comparative Culture
University of California, Irvine
Irvine, California 92717
(714) 856-5272
Director: Dickran Tashjain

University of California, Los Angeles

Chicano Studies Research Center (CSRC)

In addition to a borderlands research program conducted jointly with the Latin American Center (*see below*), the CSRC is involved in a wide range of research projects examining Mexican issues.

Chicano Studies Research Center
3121 Campbell Hall
University of California, Los Angeles
Los Angeles, California 90024
(213) 825-2363
Director: David Hayes-Bautista

Latin American Center

Founded in 1970, this center dedicates itself in part to borderlands studies. It produced *BorderLine* (Barbara G. Valk, ed.), a borderlands bibliographic data base published in book form—and no longer available on-line (*see entry in Chapter 10, section 1*). Together with the Chicano Studies Research Center, the center houses the United States–Mexico Border Research Project, which is designed to facilitate research on borderlands issues. The principal effort of the project is the collection and analysis of mappable data for the region that will be published in a multivolume *United States–Mexico Borderlands Atlas*.

Latin American Center
10343 Bunche Hall
University of California, Los Angeles
Los Angeles, California 90024
(213) 825-4571
Director: Norris Hundley

UCLA Program on Mexico

This program was founded in 1982 to coordinate research, develop faculty and student exchanges, and promote other interchanges with Mexico. Research is sponsored on a variety of subjects, including the borderlands. Work related to the border region includes two projects, both developed in conjunction with the Latin American Center: the Borderlands Atlas Project and *BorderLine*, a bibliography on the U.S.–Mexico border region.

UCLA Program on Mexico
11250 Bunche Hall
University of California, Los Angeles
Los Angeles, California 90024
(213) 206-8500
Coordinator: David E. Lorey

University of California, Riverside

UCR–Mexico Collaborative Research and Training Group

Part of the UCR Center for Social and Behavioral Science Research, this group administers, coordinates, and encourages collaborative research between Mexican scientists and UCR faculty in the social, behavioral, agricultural, and biological sciences.

UCR–Mexico Collaborative Research & Training Group
1229 Watkins Hall
University of California, Riverside
Riverside, California 92521
(714) 787-3596
Director: Robert D. Singer

University of California Consortium on Mexico and the United States (UC–MEXUS)

UC–MEXUS facilitates and coordinates research by University of California scholars—including those on campuses at Berkeley, Davis, Irvine, San Diego, Riverside, Santa Barbara, San Francisco, and Santa Cruz—

who are interested in Mexico. It also publishes a newsletter describing its activities.

UC–MEXUS
1141 Watkins Hall
University of California, Riverside
Riverside, California 92521
(714) 787-3546
Director: Arturo Gómez-Pompa

University of California, San Diego

Center for U.S.–Mexican Studies

Opened in 1980, this center combines research, instruction, publications, and public service. Its areas of interest include the economic and political relations between Mexico and the United States; the history, economy, political system, and social structure of Mexico; and aspects of U.S. public policy and the U.S. economy that affect Mexico. Among the center's publications are the *International Guide to Research on Mexico* (*see entry in Chapter 10, section 1*), and a regular publication series that includes several volumes on border affairs.

Center for U.S.–Mexican Studies
10111 North Torrey Pines Road
University of California, San Diego
La Jolla, California 92093
(619) 534-4503
Director: Wayne Cornelius

Institute of the Americas

The institute's research interests include relations between Mexico and the United States having to do with trade, energy, investment, foreign policy, migration, and the border.

131

Institute of the Americas
10111 North Torrey Pines Road
University of California, San Diego
La Jolla, California 92093
(619) 534-6052
President: Paul Boeker

UNIVERSITY OF SAN DIEGO

MEXICO–U.S. LAW INSTITUTE

The purpose of this institute is to increase knowledge of both countries' legal systems, and focus national attention on important legal issues affecting the two countries. It can provide detailed information on Mexican law firms, legislation, and governmental agencies concerned with the establishment of *maquiladora* plants in Mexico.

Mexico–U.S. Law Institute
School of Law
University of San Diego
Alcala Park
San Diego, California 92110
(619) 260-4816
Director: Jorge Vargas

COLLEGES

Imperial Valley College
P.O. Box 158
Imperial, California 92251
(619) 352-8320

Southwestern College
900 Otay Lakes Road
Chula Vista, California 92010
(619) 421-6700

New Mexico

New Mexico State University

Joint Border Research Institute (JBRI)

Established in 1978, the JBRI conducts research on U.S.–Mexico border issues, publishes the *U.S.–Mexico Report,* and handles the minutes and archives of the New Mexico Border Commission.

Joint Border Research Institute
Nason House, 1200 University
New Mexico State University
Las Cruces, New Mexico 88003
(505) 646-3524
Director: María Telles-McGeagh

University of New Mexico

International Transboundary Resources Center/Centro Internacional de Recursos Transfronterizos (CIRT)

CIRT seeks to improve policy governing the use of transboundary resources, so that such resources are distributed rationally, equitably, and cooperatively, with full respect for the territorial sovereignty of each state concerned. Although it is particularly interested in policy relating to the U.S.–Mexico border region, it also examines policy concerning other transboundary areas. CIRT publishes the *Transboundary Resources Report* (*see entry in Chapter 10, section 2*).

International Transboundary Resources Center
School of Law
University of New Mexico
Albuquerque, New Mexico 87131
(505) 277-4820
Director: Albert E. Utton

Latin American Institute (LAI)

Although the LAI does not focus primarily on border issues, it has developed and coordinated exchange programs with several different Mexican institutions.

Latin American Institute
University of New Mexico
Albuquerque, New Mexico 87131
(505) 277-2961
Director: Gilbert W. Merkx

Southwest Hispanic Research Institute

The institute's purpose is to promote teaching, research, and dissemination of information concerning historical and contemporary issues affecting Hispanics in the southwestern United States.

Southwest Hispanic Research Institute
University of New Mexico
Albuquerque, New Mexico 87131
(505) 277-2965
Director: José A. Rivera

Texas

El Paso County Community College

Center for International Programs

This center collaborates with Mexican border institutions of higher education on a number of projects.

Center for International Programs
El Paso County Community College
P.O. Box 20500
El Paso, Texas 79998
(915) 594-2419
Director: Eduardo I. Conrado

LAREDO STATE UNIVERSITY

INSTITUTE OF INTERNATIONAL TRADE

This institute, through its Border Business Indicators project, publishes business and trade statistics for the Texas–Mexico border region. The Texas legislature provides special funding for the institute to conduct studies, and to share data through periodic publications, seminars, and conferences.

Institute of International Trade
Laredo State University
West End, Washington Street
Laredo, Texas 78040
(512) 722-8001
Director: Philip Lane

TEXAS A&I UNIVERSITY

SOUTHWEST BORDERLANDS CULTURAL STUDIES AND RESEARCH CENTER

The center promotes research on ethnic minorities in the Southwest and coordinates new courses on ethnic studies offered on campus.

Southwest Borderlands Cultural Studies & Research Center
Campus Box 163
Texas A&I University
Kingsville, Texas 78363
(512) 595-2701
Director: Rosario Torres-Raines

Texas Southmost College

Border Research Program

This program's research topics include cultural change along the U.S.–Mexico border and health problems in the workplace and in the home.

Border Research Program
80 Fort Brown
Texas Southmost College
Brownsville, Texas 78520
(512) 544-8252
Director: Antonio N. Zavaleta

University of Texas at Austin

Center for Mexican American Studies (CMAS)

CMAS, established in 1970, is engaged in teaching, research, and scholarly publication in Mexican American studies. The list of CMAS books, which are distributed by University of Texas Press, contains several works dealing with the border, including the present book. CMAS also supports a wide variety of special projects, such as symposia on Tejano music (1983) and the contemporary experience of Mexican Americans in Texas (1990). Several CMAS faculty associates are engaged in research on the borderlands.

Center for Mexican American Studies
University of Texas at Austin
Austin, Texas 78712
(512) 471-4557
Director: Gilberto Cárdenas

Institute of Latin American Studies (ILAS)

ILAS, one of the oldest organizations of its type in the country, coordinates a multidisciplinary Latin American program at the University of Texas. In 1988, the institute established a Mexican Center that coordinates and promotes Mexico-related research activities, including projects that examine the U.S.–Mexico borderlands. The Cooperative Doctoral Program in Border Studies, sponsored jointly with the Center for Inter-American and Border Studies of the University of Texas at El Paso, enables graduate students to pursue doctoral studies focusing on the U.S.–Mexico border region by studying at both universities.

Institute of Latin American Studies
University of Texas at Austin
Austin, Texas 78713
(512) 471-5551
Director: Peter Cleaves

U.S.–Mexico Policy Studies Center

Focusing on both research and teaching, this center explores policy issues in the areas of international trade, migration, and political economy.

U.S.–Mexico Policy Studies Center
Lyndon B. Johnson School of Public Affairs
University of Texas at Austin
Austin, Texas 78713
(512) 471-4962
Director: Sidney Weintraub

University of Texas at El Paso (UTEP)

Center for Environmental Resource Management

Founded in 1990, this center investigates water-related subjects, including international pollution from both sides of the Rio Grande. Many existing UTEP labs are associated with the center.

Center for Environmental Resource Management
University of Texas at El Paso
El Paso, Texas 79968
(915) 747-5494
Director: Stephen Riter

CENTER FOR INTER-AMERICAN AND BORDER STUDIES

Emphasizing the study of the U.S.–Mexico border region, this center sponsors research on border-related issues and coordinates UTEP agreements with several Mexican institutions in Ciudad Juárez. A Cooperative Doctoral Program in Border Studies, sponsored jointly with the Institute of Latin American Studies of the University of Texas at Austin, enables graduate students to pursue doctoral studies focusing on the U.S.–Mexico border region by studying at both universities.

Center for Inter-American & Border Studies
University of Texas at El Paso
El Paso, Texas 79968-0605
(915) 747-5196
Director: Larry Palmer

CROSS-CULTURAL SOUTHWEST ETHNIC STUDY CENTER

This center develops courses examining value orientations, the dynamics of the interaction between different cultures, and the effect of the international border on regional life.

Cross-Cultural Southwest Ethnic Study Center
Department of Political Science
University of Texas at El Paso
El Paso, Texas 79968-0547
(915) 747-5337
Director: Z. A. Kruszewski

INSTITUTE FOR MANUFACTURING, MATERIALS, AND MANAGEMENT

The institute's primary research interest is the economic development of the borderlands, particularly the *maquiladora* industry. The institute is developing a data bank on border economic issues in conjunction with Laredo State University and the Center for Entrepreneurship and Economic Development at the University of Texas–Pan American in Edinburg.

Institute for Manufacturing, Materials, & Management
University of Texas at El Paso
El Paso, Texas 79968
(915) 747-5185
Director: Don Michie

INSTITUTE OF ORAL HISTORY

The institute maintains a collection of more than 750 oral history interviews and other materials concerning the U.S.–Mexico border—especially those pertaining to El Paso and Ciudad Juárez.

Institute of Oral History
University of Texas at El Paso
El Paso, Texas 79968
(915) 747-5508
Director: Agustín Ortega

SPECIAL COLLECTIONS, LIBRARY

The Special Collections of the UTEP library contains documents on the International Boundary and Water Commission not available elsewhere.

Special Collections, Library
University of Texas at El Paso
El Paso, Texas 79968
(915) 747-5683
Director: César Caballero

UNIVERSITY OF TEXAS–PAN AMERICAN

CENTER FOR ENTREPRENEURSHIP AND ECONOMIC DEVELOPMENT

This center was established in 1986 in order to serve as a catalyst for economic growth and diversification in the Rio Grande Valley. It is particularly interested in issues related to local *maquiladora* plants, and the unincorporated rural communities of the Valley known as *colonias*.

Center for Entrepreneurship & Economic Development
1201 West University Drive
University of Texas–Pan American
Edinburg, Texas 78539
(512) 381-3361
Director: J. Michael Patrick

OTHER COLLEGES

Laredo Junior College
West End, Washington Street
Laredo, Texas 78040
(512) 722-0521

Mexico

Baja California

COLEGIO DE LA FRONTERA NORTE (COLEF)
(*college of the northern border*)

Formerly known as Centro de Estudios Fronterizos del Norte de México (CEFNOMEX), COLEF was founded in 1982 and has rapidly become the foremost institution of higher education in either the United States or Mexico that focuses on border issues. In addition to its main location in Tijuana, it also has branches in several Mexican border cities (*see below*). COLEF conducts research, offers courses, sponsors conferences, and issues a series of publications exclusively concerned with border issues.

Colegio de la Frontera Norte
Carretera Tijuana-Ensenada, kilómetro 18
Tijuana, Baja California
Tel: 30-0411, 30-0412, 30-0413, or 30-0419
President: Jorge A. Bustamante
•*U.S. mailing address:*
 P.O. Box L
 Chula Vista, California 92012

OTHER COLLEGES AND UNIVERSITIES

MEXICALI

Centro de Enseñanza Técnica y
  Superior [CETYS]
Calzada CETYS s/n
(Apartado Postal 3-797)
21000 Mexicali, Baja California
Tel. 65-0111 through 65-0120
•*U.S. mailing address:*
 P.O. Box 2808
 Calexico, California 92231

Colegio de la Frontera Norte–
  Mexicali [COLEF Mexicali]
Calafia e Independencia
Centro Cívico, despacho 1
21000 Mexicali, Baja California
Tel: 57-2589
•*U.S. mailing address:*
 P.O. Box 5678
 Calexico, California 92231

Instituto Tecnológico de Mexicali
Prolongación Bulevar Lázaro
  Cárdenas
Colonia Elías Calles
21000 Mexicali, Baja California
Tel. 61-8522 or 61-9035

Universidad Autónoma de Baja
  California [UABC]
Avenida Alvaro Obregón y Julián
  Carrillo s/n
(Apartado Postal 459)
21100 Mexicali, Baja California
Tel. 66-2985

Universidad Pedagógica Nacional
Unidad Mexicali
Río Mocorito y José Antonio
  Torres s/n
Colonia Independencia
21000 Mexicali, Baja California
Tel. 66-2060 or 66-2080

TIJUANA

Centro de Enseñanza Técnica y
  Superior [CETYS]
Unidad Tijuana
Fraccionamiento del Lago
(Apartado Postal 4012)
22550 Tijuana, Baja California
Tel. 25-3200 or 25-3201

Centro de Investigaciones
  Históricas
Universidad Nacional Autónoma
  de Mexico–Universidad
  Autónoma de Baja California
  [UNAM–UABC]
Paseo Tijuana e Independencia
22320 Tijuana, Baja California
Tel: 83-1669

141

Instituto Tecnológico de Tijuana
Calzada del Tecnológico
Fraccionamiento Tomás de Aquino
22000 Tijuana, Baja California
Tel. 82-1439 or 82-1435

Universidad Autónoma de Baja
  California [UABC]
Unidad Tijuana
Unidad Universitaria
Ex-ejido Tampico
(Apartado Postal 267)
22000 Tijuana, Baja California
Tel. 82-1033

Universidad Iberoamericana
Plantel Noroeste
Bulevar Agua Caliente y Privada
  de los Pinos
22000 Tijuana, Baja California
Tel. 86-2014 or 86-2009

Universidad Pedagógica Nacional
Unidad Tijuana
Fresnillo 485
Colonia Cacho
32200 Tijuana, Baja California
Tel. 84-2447 or 84-2448

Chihuahua

CIUDAD JUÁREZ

Colegio de la Frontera Norte–
  Ciudad Juárez [COLEF Ciudad
  Juárez]
Edificio Centro Artesanal de
  Ciudad Juárez, mezzanine
Anillo Envolvente del PRONAF
Lincoln y Mejía
32310 Ciudad Juárez, Chihuahua
Tel. 16-8363
•*U.S. mailing address:*
  P.O. Box 1385
  El Paso, Texas 79948

Escuela Superior de Agricultura
  Hermanos Escobar, A.C.
Carretera Panamericana,
  kilómetro 12.5
(Apartado Postal 2119)
Ciudad Juárez, Chihuahua
Tel. 13-3599 or 13-3237

Instituto Tecnológico de Ciudad
  Juárez
Bulevar Tecnológico s/n
(Apartado Postal 1486, 32000)
32500 Ciudad Juárez, Chihuahua
Tel. 17-3646

Universidad Autónoma de Ciudad
  Juárez
Avenida López Mateos 20
Circuito PRONAF
(Apartado Postal 1594-D)
32300 Ciudad Juárez, Chihuahua
Tel. 16-5778 or 16-5692

Universidad Pedagógica Nacional
Unidad Ciudad Juárez
Río Efrén Ornelas
Fraccionamiento Córdoba Américas
32310 Ciudad Juárez, Chihuahua
Tel. 13-5196 or 16-7496

Coahuila

Universidad Autónoma del Noreste
Unidad Ciudad Acuña
Matamoros e Ignacio Ramírez
Ciudad Acuña, Coahuila
Tel. 2-0801

Centro Universitario del Norte
Padre de las Casas y Guerrero
Piedras Negras, Coahuila
Tel. 2-1035

Instituto Tecnológico Regional de
Piedras Negras
Avenida Tecnológica Prolongación
Poniente s/n
26080 Piedras Negras, Coahuila
Tel. 3-0135 or 3-0713

Universidad Autónoma del Noreste
Unidad Piedras Negras
Avenida E. Carranza 1300
Colonia Mundo Nuevo
Piedras Negras, Coahuila
Tel. 2-4344

Universidad Pedagógica Nacional
Unidad Piedras Negras
Xicoténcatl Norte 113
Colonia Centro
26000 Piedras Negras, Coahuila
Tel. 2-4975 or 2-4549

Sonora

Colegio de la Frontera Norte–
Nogales [COLEF Nogales]
Avenida Kennedy 8
Colonia Kennedy
Nogales, Sonora
Tel. 2-4016
•*U.S. mailing address:*
P.O. Box 3048
Nogales, Arizona 85628

Instituto Tecnológico de Nogales
Avenida de los Nogales s/n
(Apartado Postal 796)
84000 Nogales, Sonora
Tel. 2-1088 or 2-3388

Universidad Pedagógica Nacional
Unidad Nogales
Reforma Final s/n
(Apartado Postal 375)
Nogales, Sonora
Tel. 2-7355

SAN LUIS RÍO COLORADO

Universidad de San Luis Río Colorado
Carretera San Luis–Sonoita, kilómetro 6
83400 San Luis Río Colorado, Sonora
Tel. 4-1359

Tamaulipas

MATAMOROS

Colegio de la Frontera Norte–
  Matamoros [COLEF Matamoros]
Calle Sexta 17, altos
(entre Mina y Ocampo)
Matamoros, Tamaulipas
Tel. 3-4559
•U.S. mailing address:
 P.O. Box 2138
 Brownsville, Texas 78522

Instituto Tecnológico de Matamoros
Carretera Lauro Villar, kilómetro 6
(Apartado Postal 339)
87490 Matamoros, Tamaulipas
Tel. 3-9125 or 3-9177

Universidad Pedagógica Nacional
Unidad Matamoros
España esquina Plan de Ayutla,
  no. 30
Colonia Euzkadi
87370 Matamoros, Tamaulipas
Tel. 3-4720

NUEVO LAREDO

Colegio de la Frontera Norte–Nuevo
  Laredo [COLEF Nuevo Laredo]
Chihuahua 2590
Colonia Guerrero
88240 Nuevo Laredo, Tamaulipas
Tel. 5-1263
•*U.S. mailing address:*
  P.O. Box 6415
  Laredo, Texas 78042

Instituto Tecnológico de Nuevo
  Laredo
Avenida Reforma Sur 2007
(Apartado Postal 392)
88000 Nuevo Laredo, Tamaulipas
Tel. 5-3630 or 4-0915

Universidad Pedagógica Nacional
Unidad Nuevo Laredo
Orizaba 3829
Colonia México
88280 Nuevo Laredo, Tamaulipas
Tel. 4-0305 or 4-6062

Universidad Valle del Bravo
Unidad Nuevo Laredo
Anáhuac 1310
Colonia México
88280 Nuevo Laredo, Tamaulipas
Tel. 4-3020

REYNOSA

Universidad México Americana
  del Norte
Bulevar Lázaro Cárdenas 930
Colonia Anzaldúas
88630 Reynosa, Tamaulipas
Tel. 2-6406

Universidad Valle del Bravo
Victoria y Sinaloa
Colonia Rodríguez
88630 Reynosa, Tamaulipas
Tel. 2-4249 or 2-8510

9.3   PUBLIC LIBRARIES

United States

Note: Branches are listed only if they are situated outside of the city in which the main library is located.

Arizona

Cochise County Library
Old Bisbee High School
Drawer AK
Bisbee, Arizona 85603
(602) 432-5471, ext. 500

•Naco Branch
 Cochise County Library
 Box 214
 Naco, Arizona 85620

Douglas Public Library
625 Tenth Street
Douglas, Arizona 85607
(602) 364-3851

Nogales–Santa Cruz County Library
748 Grand Avenue
Nogales, Arizona 85621
(602) 287-3343, 287-2911

Sierra Vista Public Library
2950 East Tacoma
Sierra Vista, Arizona 85635
(602) 458-4225

Tucson Public Library
110 East Pennington
(P.O. Box 27470)
Tucson, Arizona 85726
(602) 791-4391

Yuma County Library
350 Third Avenue
Yuma, Arizona 85364
(602) 782-1871

•San Luis Branch
 Yuma County Library
 P.O. Box 1
 San Luis, Arizona 85349
 (602) 627-8143

•Somerton Branch
 Yuma County Library
 P.O. Box 635
 Somerton, Arizona 85350
 (602) 627-2149

California

Brawley Public Library
400 Main Street
Brawley, California 92227
(619) 344-1891

Enrique S. "Kiki" Camarena
    Memorial Library
850 Encinas Avenue
Calexico, California 92231
(619) 357-2605

Meyer Memorial Library
225 West Main
Calipatria, California 92233
(619) 348-2630

Chula Vista Public Library
365 F Street
Chula Vista, California 92010
(619) 691-5168

El Centro Public Library
539 State Street
El Centro, California 92243
(619) 352-0751

Imperial County Free Library
1647 West Main
El Centro, California 92243
(619) 353-3500

Meyer Memorial Library
101 East Sixth Street
Holtville, California 92247
(619) 356-2385

Imperial Public Library
200 West Ninth Street
Imperial, California 92251
(619) 355-1332

National City Public Library
200 East Twelfth Street
National City, California 92050
(619) 474-8211

San Diego County Library
5555 Overland Avenue, bldg. 15
San Diego, California 92123
(619) 694-2414

•Imperial Beach Branch
 San Diego County Library
 810 Imperial Beach Blvd.
 Imperial Beach, California 92032
 (619) 424-6981

•Lincoln Acres Branch
 San Diego County Library
 2725 Granger Avenue
 National City, California 92050
 (619) 475-9880

•Woodlawn Park Branch
 San Diego County Library
 115 Spruce Road
 Chula Vista, California 92011
 (619) 426-8111

San Diego Public Library
820 E Street
San Diego, California 92101
(619) 236-5800

•Otay Mesa Branch
 San Diego Public Library
 3003 Coronado Avenue
 Otay Mesa, California 92154
 (619) 424-5871

•San Ysidro Branch
San Diego Public Library
101 West San Ysidro Blvd.
San Ysidro, California 92073
(619) 428-2111

New Mexico

Thomas Branigan Memorial Library
Las Cruces Public Library
200 East Picacho Avenue
Las Cruces, New Mexico 88001
(505) 526-1047

Texas

Alpine Public Library
203 North Seventh Street
Alpine, Texas 79830
(915) 837-2621

Arnulfo L. Oliveira Memorial
   Library
1825 May Street
Brownsville, Texas 78520
(512) 544-8221

South Texas Library System
805 Comanche Street
Corpus Christi, Texas 78401
(512) 880-8915
•*Member libraries include:*
   Brownsville, Donna, Edinburg,
   Harlingen, La Feria, Laredo, Los
   Fresnos, McAllen, Mercedes, Mis-
   sion, Pharr, San Benito, Weslaco

Val Verde County Library
300 Spring Street
Del Rio, Texas 78840
(512) 774-3622

Eagle Pass Public Library
589 Main
Eagle Pass, Texas 78852
(512) 773-1915

Edinburg Public Library
401 East Cano
Edinburg, Texas 78539
(512) 383-6246

El Paso Public Library
501 North Oregon Street
El Paso, Texas 79901
(915) 541-4864

Harlingen Public Library
504 East Tyler Avenue
Lon C. Hill Memorial Bldg.
Harlingen, Texas 78550
(512) 427-8841

Hidalgo County Library System
4305 North Tenth Street, suite E
McAllen, Texas 78504
(512) 682-6397
•*Member libraries include:*
Alamo, Donna, Edinburg, Elsa,
Mercedes, Mission, Pharr, Weslaco

McAllen Memorial Library
601 North Main Street
McAllen, Texas 78501
(512) 682-4531

Laredo Public Library
Bruni Plaza
Laredo, Texas 78040
(512) 722-2435

Zapata County Public Library
901 Kennedy Street
(P.O. Box 2806)
Zapata, Texas 78076
(512) 765-5351

Mexico

The Mexican public library system has recently been reorganized under the directorship of Dr. Ana María Magaloni. The public library coordinators for each Mexican border state are listed first, followed by the public libraries in border cities and towns.

Baja California

Lic. Juana Mosqueda Loeza
Coordinadora de Bibliotecas
Biblioteca Pública Central del Estado, No. 190
Avenida Obregón y Calle E, no. 1300
21100 Mexicali, Baja California
Tel. 52-6195

MEXICALI

Biblioteca Escolar Granja
  Orientación, No. 2466
Colonia Ahumada s/n
Mexicali, Baja California

Biblioteca Pública Central, No. 190
Avenida Obregón y Calle E, no. 1300
21100 Mexicali, Baja California
Tel. 52-6195

Biblioteca Pública Francisco I.
  Madero, No. 4451
(Academia Estatal de Policía)
Avenida Zacatecana y Teul, no. 828
Ex-ejido Zacatecas
21090 Mexicali, Baja California
Tel. 57-0535

Instituto de Cultura de Baja
  California
Calle Obregón 1209
Mexicali, Baja California
Tel. 53-5044 or 53-5303

TECATE

Biblioteca Pública Benito Juárez, No. 1983
Sección Luis Jiménez Espinoza
Vicente Guerrero y Abelardo L. Rodríguez
Colonia Militar
21470 Tecate, Baja California
Tel. 4-1176

TIJUANA

Biblioteca Pública Teniente
  Guerrero, No. 2
Calle G s/n
22000 Tijuana, Baja California
Tel. 84-2691

Biblioteca Pública Benito Juárez,
  No. 347
Paseo Tijuana 460, Zona Río
22320 Tijuana, Baja California
Tel. 84-2691

Biblioteca Lic. Adolfo López
  Mateos, No. 4074
Playas de Rosarito
Tijuana, Baja California

Biblioteca Pública José María
  Morelos y Pavón, No. 2646
Playas de Tijuana
22200 Tijuana, Baja California

Biblioteca Pública Josefa Ortiz de
  Domínguez, No. 2644
Casa de la Cultura
Lisboa y París, no. 5
Colonia Altamira
22120 Tijuana, Baja California
Tel. 87-2604

Biblioteca Pública Primo Tapia,
  No. 2723
Ejido Primo Tapia
Tijuana, Baja California

Biblioteca Pública Dr. Gustavo
  Aubanel Vallejo, No. 4073
Parque Club Soroptimista
Fraccionamiento Contreras de la
  Mesa
Tijuana, Baja California

Chihuahua

Lic. Gaspar Gumaro Orozco
Coordinador Estatal de Bibliotecas
Director, Centro de Información del CIDECH
Universidad y División del Norte, no. 1522
31170 Chihuahua, Chihuahua
Tel. 13-4806, 13-6249, or 13-6252

CIUDAD JUÁREZ

Biblioteca Pública Municipal
Carretera Juárez-Porvenir,
 kilómetro 29, San Agustín
32720 Ciudad Juárez, Chihuahua
Tel. 14-9930

Biblioteca Pública Municipal Benito
 Juárez
Sanders y Sevilla
Colonia San Antonio
32250 Ciudad Juárez, Chihuahua
Tel. 13-6983

Biblioteca Pública Arturo Tolentino
Ignacio Ramírez 353
32000 Ciudad Juárez, Chihuahua
Tel. 13-6983

OJINAGA

Biblioteca Pública José Leyva Aguilar
Zaragoza y Segunda
32880 Ojinaga, Chihuahua
Tel. 145 [caseta]

IGNACIO ZARAGOZA

Biblioteca Pública Prof. José Santos Valdez
31920 Ignacio Zaragoza, Chihuahua
Tel. 3-0115

Coahuila

Prof. Ramiro del Bosque Celestino
Coordinador de Bibliotecas del Estado de Coahuila
Dirección General de Educación y Cultura
Bulevar Francisco Coss y Purcell
25000 Saltillo, Coahuila
Tel. 4-4989

LIBRARIES

Biblioteca Pública Municipal Lic.
 Elsa Hernández de las Fuentes
Guerrero Sur 800
26200 Ciudad Acuña, Coahuila
Tel. 2-3598

Biblioteca Pública No. 4
Avenida López Mateos 800
Colonia Roma
26000 Piedras Negras, Coahuila
Tel. 2-4662 or 2-0579

Biblioteca Pública Prof. Jorge
 Cervera Sánchez
Presidencia Municipal
26640 Guerrero, Coahuila
Tel. 1-1401

Nuevo León

Lic. Rolando Guzmán Flores
Coordinador del Sistema Estatal de Museos y Bibliotecas
Dirección General de Educación y Cultura
Zaragoza y Corregidora
Bajos del Antiguo Palacio Municipal
Monterrey, Nuevo León
Tel. 44-2503

LIBRARIES

Biblioteca Pública Municipal Lic. Nemecio García Naranjo
Plaza Municipal Juárez
Municipio Anáhuac
65030 Congregación Colombia, Nuevo León
Tel. 7-0045

Sonora

Prof. Elías Acuña Coronado
Coordinador de Bibliotecas
Dirección de Bibliotecas en el Estado
Edificio Sonora, 1er piso, departamento 113
(Pedro Moreno y Serdán final) Colonia Centro
83000 Hermosillo, Sonora
Tel. 6-1527, 3-2704, or 7-0508

LIBRARIES

Biblioteca Pública ISSSTE–SEP,
  No. 1632
Avenida Cuarta y Calle Sexta,
  no. 640
84200 Agua Prieta, Sonora
Tel. 8-1723

Biblioteca Pública Enriqueta de
  Parodi, No. 2970
Avenida Madero s/n
84180 Naco, Sonora
Tel. 4-0236

Biblioteca Pública Prof. Alfonso
  Acosta Villalvazo, No. 359
Avenida Obregón 1561
84000 Nogales, Sonora
Tel. 2-3249

Biblioteca Pública Prof. Adalberto
  Sotelo ISSSTE–SEP, No. 324
Avenida Hidalgo y Calle Diez
San Luis Río Colorado, Sonora
Tel. 4-1763

Biblioteca Pública Carolina Zepeda,
  No. 3058
Calle Hidalgo 18
84140 Santa Cruz, Sonora
Tel. 2-5816

Biblioteca Pública Dr. Rafael Cota
  Amao, No. 1856
Benito Juárez s/n
83570 Sonoita, Sonora
Tel. 2-1092

Tamaulipas

Lic. Guillermo Acevedo Ruelas
Coordinador de la Red Estatal de Bibliotecas
Dirección General de Educación y Cultura
Torre Gubernamental, 9° piso
87000 Ciudad Victoria, Tamaulipas
Tel. 2-8554 or 2-8766

LIBRARIES

Biblioteca Pública Francisco Bada
  López
Calle Hidalgo s/n
Casa de la Cultura
88390 Ciudad Mier, Tamaulipas
Tel. 3-0070 or 3-0071

Biblioteca Pública Lic. Lauro
  Rendón Valdez
88400 Gustavo Díaz Ordaz,
  Tamaulipas
Tel. 8-2053 or 8-2417

Biblioteca Pública Agapito González
  Cavazos
Iturbide y Dozava, no. 95, 2º piso
87300 Matamoros, Tamaulipas
Tel. 3-6044, 2-0650, or 3-9809

Biblioteca Pública Prof. Juan B.
  Tijerina
Avenida Universidad s/n
Parque Manatou
87380 Matamoros, Tamaulipas
Tel. 3-6044, 2-0650, or 3-9809

Biblioteca Pública Prof. Miguel
  Díaz de la Cruz
Francisco I. Madero y Zapata
Plaza Hidalgo
83000 Miguel Alemán, Tamaulipas
Tel. 2-0148 or 2-0935

Biblioteca Pública José Bernardo
  Gutiérrez de Lara
Vicente Guerrero y Eisenhower
Plaza Pública
88370 Nueva Ciudad Guerrero,
  Tamaulipas
Tel. 6-0370 or 6-0114 [Presidencia
  Municipal]

Biblioteca Pública José Vasconcelos
Plaza México s/n
88000 Nuevo Laredo, Tamaulipas
Tel. 2-4580, 2-8554, or 2-3020

Biblioteca Pública Prof. Agapito
  Cepeda Uriegas
Saltillo 555
Colonia Longoria
88660 Reynosa, Tamaulipas
Tel. 2-0005 or 2-1168

Biblioteca Pública Año de la Patria
Madero s/n
Interior de Casa de la Cultura
87000 Río Bravo, Tamaulipas
Tel. 4-0011 or 4-3033

10 BORDER STUDIES BIBLIOGRAPHY

10.1 BIBLIOGRAPHIES AND OTHER REFERENCE WORKS

American Chamber of Commerce of Mexico. *Mexico's Maquiladora In-Bond Industry Handbook.* 8th ed. México, D.F.: AMCHAM, 1991.

Designed for the U.S. business community, this handbook contains an excellent overview of the *maquiladora* industry, as well as detailed descriptions of how to set up a *maquiladora* operation. Useful appendixes include lists of Mexican government offices, consultants, customs brokers, and promoters.

Bustamante, Jorge A., and Francisco Malagamba. *México–Estados Unidos: Bibliografía general sobre estudios fronterizos.* México, D.F.: Colegio de México, 1980.

Monographs, books, journal articles, theses and dissertations, and professional papers are included in this bibliography, which primarily covers the border literature of the 1970s. Both Mexican and U.S. sources are listed, arranged by broad subject area.

Caballero, César, comp. *The Border Finder: A Border Studies Bibliography.* Book 1. El Paso: The Library, University of Texas at El Paso, 1987.

This serial bibliography is a selective listing of significant books, journals, and articles on border issues. Entries are annotated and a subject/key-word index is included.

Center for U.S.–Mexican Studies, University of California, San Diego, and Colegio de la Frontera Norte. *International Guide to Research on Mexico/Guía Internacional de Investigaciones sobre México.* La Jolla, Calif.: CUSMS; and Tijuana: COLEF; 1986–. Biennial.

Published in association with the University of California Consortium on Mexico and the United States (UC–MEXUS), this collaborative effort represents a "comprehensive inventory of ongoing Mexico-related research." A section on border studies is included, along with indexes by subject and name of researcher.

Cumberland, Charles C. *The United States–Mexican Border: A Selective Guide to the Literature of the Region.* Ithaca, N.Y.: Rural Sociological Society, 1960.

Published as a supplement to the journal *Rural Sociology* (vol. 25, June 1960), this pioneering work consists of bibliographic essays on major topics related to the border such as education, culture, Indians, and diplomatic relations. Books, monographs, journal articles, government publications, theses, and unpublished manuscripts are discussed.

Lorey, David E., ed. *United States–Mexico Border Statistics since 1900*. Los Angeles: Latin American Center, University of California, Los Angeles, 1990.

The "first comprehensive collection of historical statistics on the border," this new reference book provides data on most aspects of life on both sides of the border. Statistical material is divided into four major parts: "Life on the Border," "Work and Migration," "The Border Economy," and "Trade, Tourism, and Finance."

Mexico Communications. *Directory of In-Bond Plants (Maquiladoras) in Mexico*. El Paso: MC, 1984–. Annual.

Arranged by city and state, this directory lists the *maquiladora*'s name, address, and phone number; the name of its executive or manager; and its product or services, plant size, and number of workers.

Peña, Devón Gerardo. *Maquiladoras: A Select Annotated Bibliography and Critical Commentary on the United States–Mexico Border Industry Program*. CSHR Bibliography Series, no. 7-81. Austin: Center for the Study of Human Resources, University of Texas at Austin, 1981.

This bibliography contains lengthy descriptive annotations of major articles and monographs on the *maquiladora* industry published through 1980. Mexican sources are well represented.

Pick, James B., Edgar W. Butler, and Elizabeth L. Lanzer. *Atlas of Mexico*. Boulder, Colo.: Westview Press, 1989.

This atlas contains a wealth of economic and demographic data on Mexican border municipalities and states, as well as data on federal election results.

Reich, Peter L., ed. *Statistical Abstract of the United States–Mexico Borderlands*. Los Angeles: Latin American Center Publications, University of California, Los Angeles, 1984.

This work "constitutes a first effort to present binational quantitative time series for the Mexico–United States borderlands region." It includes short articles related to quantitative techniques.

San Diego Association of Governments. *The Bridge: Baja California Regional Industrial Development Guide.* San Diego: SANDAG, 1988.

A cooperative effort of the county of San Diego's Department of Transborder Affairs, the city of San Diego's Department of Binational Affairs, the San Diego Economic Development Corporation, and the San Diego Association of Governments, this work is a "resource guide to demographics and industrial development, with particular reference to the *maquiladora* . . . program in the border region of Baja California, especially Tijuana."

Sklair, Leslie. *Maquiladoras: An Annotated Bibliography and Research Guide to Mexico's In-Bond Industry, 1980–1988.* Monograph Series, no. 24. La Jolla, Calif.: Center for U.S.–Mexican Studies, University of California, San Diego, 1988.

This work includes annotations for published and unpublished academic literature on *maquiladoras* in the 1980s, newspaper and magazine articles, and "political and promotional materials." It is an extremely useful guide to the burgeoning literature on the *maquiladora* industry.

Stoddard, Ellwyn R., Richard L. Nostrand, and Jonathan P. West, eds. *Borderlands Sourcebook: A Guide to the Literature on Northern Mexico and the American Southwest.* Norman, Okla.: University of Oklahoma Press, 1983.

Three sections of bibliographic essays written by subject specialists cover all facets of U.S.–Mexico border studies. A lengthy bibliography and index are included.

U.S. General Accounting Office. *Immigration: Studies of the Immigration and Control Act's Impact on Mexico.* Briefing Report to the Honorable Dennis DeConcini, U.S. Senate. GAO/NSAID-88-92BR. Washington, D.C.: GAO, 1988.

This briefing report summarizes the possible effects of IRCA on the Mexican economy. It includes an annotated bibliography of studies that provide "baseline data on emigration from Mexico to the United States."

Valk, Barbara G., ed. *BorderLine: A Bibliography of the United States–Mexico Borderlands.* Los Angeles: Latin American Center, University of California, Los Angeles, and the University of California Consortium on Mexico and the United States, 1987.

This comprehensive and monumental bibliography, "encompass[ing] all major academic disciplines," includes books, chapters of books, journal articles, manuscripts, government documents, conference proceedings, unpublished papers, maps, and audiovisual material. It is arranged by subject and includes an author index.

10.2 JOURNALS AND NEWSLETTERS

Border Health/Salud Fronteriza. El Paso: United States–Mexico Border Health Association, vol. 1, no. 1 (1985)––. Quarterly.

This bilingual journal is devoted to "shar[ing] experiences and knowledge along the border in the field of health." Articles are understandable to the lay reader and cover a wide range of topics, such as epidemiology, community health care, prenatal health, immigrant health service, and folk medicine.

Borderlands Journal. Brownsville, Tex.: South Texas Institute of Latin and Mexican American Research, Texas Southmost College, vol. 3, no. 2 (Spring 1980)––. Biannual.

This interdisciplinary journal was formerly known as the *South Texas Journal of Research and Humanities.*

Border Trax. El Paso: Border Trax, Inc., vol. 4, no. 1 (January 1991)––. Monthly.

Geared to U.S.–based enterprises trading with Mexico, this magazine covers all aspects of border business. It is also available in audiocassette format.

Correo Fronterizo. Tijuana: Colegio de la Frontera Norte, año 1, no. 1 (marzo–abril 1986)––. Bimonthly.

The official newsletter of the Colegio de la Frontera Norte (COLEF), it was previously known as *Boletín CEFNOMEX,* which was the newsletter of the Centro de Estudios Fronterizos del Norte de México (COLEF's previous name).

Cultura Norte. México, D.F.: Programa Cultural de las Fronteras, Secretaría de Educación Pública, vol. 1, no. 1 (julio–agosto 1987)––. Bimonthly.

Cosponsored by the seven Mexican border states, this Spanish-language magazine contains articles intended for the general reader on social, historical, and cultural aspects of border life.

Estudios Fronterizos: Revista del Instituto de Investigaciones Sociales. Mexicali: Universidad Autónoma de Baja California, año 1, no. 1 (mayo–agosto 1983)—. Triannual.

This journal covers a wide range of topics, including economic development, migration, politics, and cultural identity, and is not limited in subject matter to the U.S.–Mexico border area. It regularly reprints historical documents such as treaties and other international agreements.

Frontera Norte. Tijuana: Colegio de la Frontera Norte, vol. 1, no. 1 (enero–junio 1989)—. Biannual.

This bilingual journal includes scholarly articles, essays, and book reviews examining U.S. and Mexican border issues.

Journal of Borderlands Studies. Las Cruces, N.Mex.: New Mexico State University, vol. 1, no. 1 (Spring 1986)—. Biannual.

This journal focuses on the U.S.–Mexico border region, and occasionally contains articles examining other international borders. It is cosponsored by the Association of Borderlands Scholars.

Mexico Policy News. San Diego: Institute for Regional Studies of the Californias, San Diego State University, no. 1 (Spring 1986)—. Annual.

The newsletter of the Consortium of U.S. Research Programs for Mexico (PROFMEX), it reports on current research, conferences, and publications of participating academic institutions.

Natural Resources Journal. Albuquerque: School of Law, University of New Mexico, vol. 1 (March 1961)—. Quarterly.

This journal is a regular source of scholarly articles on transboundary environmental concerns, occasionally devoting entire issues to the topic.

News/Noticias. El Paso: Pan American Health Organization and U.S.–Mexico Border Health Association, no. 1 (1984?)—. Quarterly.

This newsletter provides information on border health and health-care issues to the association's membership.

Río Bravo: A Journal of Research and Issues. Edinburg, Tex.: Center for International Studies, University of Texas–Pan American, vol. 1, no. 1 (Summer 1991)—. Quarterly.

This new interdisciplinary and bilingual journal will focus on border issues of special interest to the Texas–Mexico borderlands.

Southwestern Review of Management and Economics. Albuquerque: Institute for Applied Research Services, University of New Mexico, vol. 1, no. 1 (1981)—. Quarterly.

This journal regularly devotes space to border topics such as immigration, the border economy, and the border environment.

Transboundary Resources Report. Albuquerque: Transboundary Resources Center, School of Law, University of New Mexico, vol. 1, no. 1 (Spring 1987)—. Triannual.

Issues pertaining to transboundary air, water, and waste are the focus of this newsletter. It concentrates on the U.S.–Mexico borderlands, although other border regions are discussed as well.

Twin Plant News. El Paso: Nibbe, Hernández, and Associates, vol. 1, no. 1 (August 1985)—. Monthly.

Subtitled "The Magazine of the Maquiladora Industry," this publication is addressed specifically to U.S. managers and executives. It features articles on *maquiladora* products, labor, and legislation, and highlights individual *maquiladoras.*

U.S.–Mexico Report. Las Cruces, N.Mex.: New Mexico Border Commission, with Joint Border Research Institute and Center for Latin American Studies, New Mexico State University, vol. 1, no. 1 (November 1984)—. Monthly.

Articles discussing the border are selected from major Mexican newspapers and translated for English-language readers. They are arranged chronologically.

10.3 GENERAL WORKS

Applegate, Howard G., and C. Richard Bath, eds. *Air Pollution along the United States–Mexican Border.* El Paso: Texas Western Press, 1974.

Ashabranner, Brent K. *The Vanishing Border: A Photographic Journey along Our Frontier with Mexico.* Photographs by Paul Conklin. New York: Dodd, Mead, 1987.

Baerresen, Donald. *The Border Industrialization Program of Mexico.* Lexington, Mass.: Heath-Lexington, 1971.

Baird, Peter, and Ed McCaughan. *Beyond the Border: Mexico and the U.S. Today.* New York: North American Congress on Latin America, 1979.

Barrera, Mario. *Race and Class in the Southwest: A Theory of Racial Inequality.* Notre Dame, Ind.: University of Notre Dame Press, 1979.

Bartlett, John R. *Personal Narrative of Explorations and Incidents in Texas, New Mexico, California, Sonora, and Chihuahua, connected with the United States and Mexican Boundary Commission during the Years 1850–53.* Chicago: Rio Grande Press, 1965.

Bilateral Commission on the Future of United States–Mexican Relations. *The Challenge of Interdependence: Managing the Relationship between Mexico and the United States.* Berkeley, Calif.: University of California Press, 1988.

Brannon, Jeffery T., and David A. Schnauer. *Financial Institutions in El Paso, Texas, and Ciudad Juárez, Chihuahua: A Comparative Analysis.* El Paso: Center for Inter-American and Border Studies, University of Texas at El Paso, 1984.

Brown, Peter G., and Henry Shue, eds. *The Border that Joins: Mexican Migrants and U.S. Responsibility.* Totowa, N.J.: Rowman and Littlefield, 1983.

―――. *Boundaries, National Autonomy, and Its Limits.* Totowa, N.J.: Rowman and Littlefield, 1981.

Bustamante, Jorge A. *Espaldas mojadas: Materia prima para la expansión del capital norteamericano.* México, D.F.: Colegio de México, 1975.

Carrillo, Jorge, comp. *Reestructuración industrial: Maquiladoras en la frontera México–Estados Unidos.* México, D.F.: Secretaría de Educación Pública; and Tijuana: Colegio de la Frontera Norte; 1989.

Carrillo V., Jorge, and Alberto Hernández. *Mujeres fronterizas en la industria maquiladora.* México, D.F.: Secretaría de Educación Pública; and Tijuana: Centro de Estudios Fronterizos del Norte de México; 1985.

Chan, Linda S., and David C. Warner. *Maternal and Child Health on the U.S.–Mexico Border.* Special Project Report. Austin: Lyndon Baines Johnson School of Public Affairs, University of Texas at Austin, 1987.

Clement, Norris C. *Maquiladora Resource Guide: Exploring the Maquiladora/In-Bond Option in Baja California, Mexico.* San Diego: Institute for Regional Studies of the Californias, San Diego State University, 1989.

Clifford, Roy A. *The Rio Grande Flood: A Comparative Study of Border Communities in Disaster.* National Resource Council Publication no. 458. Washington, D.C.: National Academy of Sciences–National Research Council, 1956.

Cockcroft, James D. *Outlaws in the Promised Land: Mexican Immigrant Workers and America's Future.* New York: Grove Press, 1985.

Coerver, Don M., and Linda B. Hall. *Texas and the Mexican Revolution: A Study in State and National Border Policy, 1910–1920.* San Antonio: Trinity University Press, 1984.

Conover, Ted. *Coyotes: A Journey through the Secret World of America's Illegal Aliens.* New York: Vintage, 1987.

Cornelius, Wayne A. *Mexican Migration to the United States: The View from Rural Sending Communities.* Cambridge, Mass.: Migration and

Development Study Group, Center for International Studies, Massachusetts Institute of Technology, 1976.

Cornelius, Wayne A., and Ricardo Anzaldúa Montoya, eds. *America's New Immigration Law: Origins, Rationales, and Potential Consequences.* La Jolla, Calif.: Center for U.S.–Mexican Studies, University of California, San Diego, 1983.

Craig, Richard B. *The Bracero Program: Interest Groups and Foreign Policy.* Austin: University of Texas Press, 1971.

Crewdson, John. *The Tarnished Door: The New Immigrants and the Transformation of America.* New York: Times Books, 1983.

Cross, Harry E., and James A. Sandos. *Across the Border: Rural Development in Mexico and Recent Migration to the United States.* Berkeley, Calif.: Institute of Governmental Studies, University of California, Berkeley, 1981.

D'Antonio, William V., and William H. Form. *Influentials in Two Border Cities.* Notre Dame, Ind.: University of Notre Dame Press, 1965.

Demaris, Ovid. *Poso del Mundo: Inside the Mexican American Border from Tijuana to Matamoros.* Boston: Little, Brown, 1970.

Diez-Cañedo Ruiz, Juan. *La migración indocumentada de México a los Estados Unidos: Un nuevo enfoque.* México, D.F.: Fondo de Cultura Económica, 1984.

Eaton, David J., and John M. Andersen. *The State of the Rio Grande/Río Bravo: A Study of Water Resource Issues along the Texas/Mexico Border.* Tucson: University of Arizona Press, 1987.

Ehrlich, Paul R., Loy Bilderback, and Anne H. Ehrlich. *The Golden Door: International Migration, Mexico, and the United States.* New York: Ballantine Books, 1979.

Emory, William H. *Report on the United States and Mexican Boundary Survey, Made under the Direction of the Secretary of the Interior.*

Washington, D.C.: C. Wendell, Printer, 1857–59. 3 vols. Reprint. Austin: Texas State Historical Association, 1987.

Fatemi, Khosrow, ed. *Maquiladora Industry: Economic Solution or Problem?* New York: Praeger, 1990.

Fernández, Raúl A. *The Mexican-American Border Region: Issues and Trends.* Notre Dame, Ind.: University of Notre Dame Press, 1989.

———. *The United States–Mexico Border: A Politico-Economic Profile.* Notre Dame, Ind.: University of Notre Dame Press, 1977.

Fernández-Kelly, María Patricia. *For We Are Sold, I and My People: Women and Industry in Mexico's Frontier.* Albany: State University of New York Press, 1983.

Fowler, Gene, and Bill Crawford. *Border Radio.* Austin: University of Texas Press, 1988.

Ganster, Paul, ed. *The Maquiladora Program in Trinational Perspective: Mexico, Japan, and the United States.* San Diego: Institute for Regional Studies of the Californias, San Diego State University, 1987.

García, Juan Ramón. *Operation Wetback: The Mass Deportation of Mexican Undocumented Workers in 1954.* Westport, Conn.: Greenwood Press, 1980.

García, Mario T. *Desert Immigrants: The Mexicans of El Paso, 1880–1920.* New Haven, Conn.: Yale University Press, 1981.

Garreau, Joel. *The Nine Nations of North America.* Boston: Houghton Mifflin, 1981.

Gehlbach, Frederick R. *Mountain Islands and Desert Seas: A Natural History of the U.S.–Mexican Borderlands.* College Station, Tex.: Texas A&M University Press, 1981.

Gibson, Lay James, and Alfonso Corona-Rentería, eds. *The U.S. and Mexico: Borderland Development and the National Economies.* Boulder, Colo.: Westview Press, 1985.

González-Aréchiga, Bernardo, and Rocío Barajas Escamilla, comps. *Las maquiladoras: Ajuste estructural y desarrollo regional.* Tijuana: Colegio de la Frontera Norte and Fundación Friedrich Ebert, 1989.

González Salazar, Roque, ed. *La frontera del norte: Integración y desarrollo.* México, D.F.: Colegio de México, 1981.

Hall, Douglas Kent. *The Border: Life on the Line.* New York: Abbeville Press, 1988.

Hall, Linda B., and Don M. Coerver. *Revolution on the Border: The United States and Mexico, 1910–1920.* Albuquerque: University of New Mexico Press, 1988.

Hansen, Niles. *The Border Economy: Regional Development in the Southwest.* Austin: University of Texas Press, 1981.

Harris, Charles H. III, and Louis R. Sadler. *The Border and the Revolution.* Las Cruces, N.Mex.: Center for Latin American Studies and Joint Border Research Institute, New Mexico State University, 1988.

Herzog, Lawrence A. *Where North Meets South: Cities, Space, and Politics on the U.S.–Mexico Border.* Austin: Center for Mexican American Studies, University of Texas at Austin, 1990.

Hine, Robert V. *Bartlett's West: Drawing the Mexican Boundary.* New Haven, Conn.: Yale University Press, 1968.

Hinojosa, Gilberto Miguel. *A Borderlands Town in Transition: Laredo, 1755–1870.* College Station, Tex.: A&M University Press, 1983.

Horgan, Paul. *Great River.* New York: Holt, Rinehart & Winston, 1954. 2 vols. Reprint. Austin: Texas Monthly Press, 1984.

House, John W. *Frontier on the Rio Grande: A Political Geography of Development and Social Deprivation.* Oxford: Clarendon Press, 1982.

Human Resources Agency. County of San Diego. *A Study of the Socioeconomic Impact of Illegal Aliens on the County of San Diego.* San Diego: HRA, 1977.

Humphrey, Robert R. *90 Years and 535 Miles: Vegetation Changes along the Mexican Border.* Albuquerque: University of New Mexico Press, 1987.

Hundley, Norris. *Dividing the Waters: A Century of Controversy between the United States and Mexico.* Berkeley, Calif.: University of California Press, 1966.

Iglesias, Norma. *La flor más bella de la maquiladora: Historia de vida de la mujer obrera en Tijuana, Baja California.* México, D.F.: Secretaría de Educación Pública; and Tijuana: Centro de Estudios Fronterizos del Norte de México; 1985.

International Boundary and Water Commission, United States and Mexico. *Joint Projects of the United States and Mexico through the International Boundary and Water Commission.* El Paso: IBWC, 1981.

Klagsbrunn, Víctor, ed. *Tijuana: Cambio social y migración.* Tijuana: Colegio de la Frontera Norte, 1988.

Knowlton, Clark S., ed. *International Water Law along the Mexican-American Border.* El Paso: Texas Western Press, 1968.

Lamborn, Alan C., and Stephen P. Mumme. *Statecraft, Domestic Politics, and Foreign Policy Making: The El Chamizal Dispute.* Boulder, Colo.: Westview Press, 1988.

Margulis, Mario, and Rodolfo Tuirán. *Desarrollo y población en la frontera norte: El caso de Reynosa.* México, D.F.: Colegio de México, 1986.

Martínez, Oscar J. *Border Boom Town: Ciudad Juárez since 1948.* Austin: University of Texas Press, 1973.

———. *The Foreign Orientation of the Mexican Border Economy.* El Paso: Center for Inter-American and Border Studies, University of Texas at El Paso, 1983.

———. *Troublesome Border.* Tucson: University of Arizona Press, 1988.

Martínez, Oscar J., Albert E. Utton, and Mario Miranda Pacheco. *One Border, Two Nations: Policy Implications and Problem Resolutions.* Fourth

Symposium of Mexican and United States Universities on Border Studies, sponsored by PROFMEX and ANUIES. México, D.F.: Asociación de Universidades e Institutos de Enseñanza Superior, 1988.

Metz, Leon C. *Border: The U.S.–Mexico Line.* El Paso: Mangan Books, 1989.

Miller, Michael V. *Economic Growth and Change along the U.S.–Mexican Border: The Case of Brownsville, Texas.* Austin: Bureau of Business Research, University of Texas at Austin, 1982.

Miller, Tom. *On the Border.* New York: Harper & Row, 1981.

Nalven, Joseph. *Impacts and Undocumented Persons: The Quest for Useable Data in San Diego County, 1974–1986.* San Diego: Institute for Regional Studies of the Californias, San Diego State University, 1986.

Ojeda, Mario. *Administración del desarrollo de la frontera norte.* México, D.F.: Colegio de México, 1982.

———. *Mexico: The Northern Border as a National Concern.* El Paso: Center for Inter-American and Border Studies, University of Texas at El Paso, 1983.

Paredes, Américo. *"With His Pistol in His Hand": A Border Ballad and Its Hero.* Austin: University of Texas Press, 1958.

Piñera Ramírez, David. *Historia de Tijuana: Semblanza general.* Tijuana: Centro de Investigaciones Históricas, Universidad Nacional Autónoma de México–Universidad Autónoma de Baja California, 1985.

Price, John A. *Tijuana: Urbanization in a Border Culture.* Notre Dame, Ind.: University of Notre Dame Press, 1973.

Price, Thomas J. *Standoff at the Border: A Failure of Microdiplomacy.* El Paso: Texas Western Press, 1989.

Riding, Alan. *Distant Neighbors: A Portrait of the Mexicans.* New York: Alfred A. Knopf, 1985.

Rosenthal-Urey, Ina. *Regional Impacts of U.S.–Mexican Relations.* La Jolla, Calif.: Center for U.S.–Mexican Studies, University of California, San Diego, 1986.

Ross, Stanley R., ed. *Views across the Border: The United States and Mexico.* Albuquerque: University of New Mexico Press, 1978.

Ruiz, Vicki L., and Susan Tiano, eds. *Women on the U.S.–Mexico Border: Responses to Change.* Boston: Allen & Unwin, 1987.

Seligson, Mitchell A., and Edward J. Williams. *Maquiladoras and Migration: Workers in the Mexico–United States Border Industrialization Program.* Austin: Mexico–U.S. Border Research Program, University of Texas at Austin, 1981.

Sepúlveda, César, and Albert E. Utton, eds. *The U.S.–Mexico Border Region: Anticipating Resource Needs and Issues to the Year 2000.* El Paso: Texas Western Press, and Center for Inter-American and Border Studies, University of Texas at El Paso, 1984.

Sklair, Leslie. *Assembling for Development: The Maquila Industry in Mexico and the United States.* Winchester, Mass.: Unwin Hyman, 1989.

Spicer, Edward H. *Cycles of Conquest: The Impact of Spain, Mexico, and the United States on the Indians of the Southwest, 1533–1960.* Tucson: University of Arizona Press, 1962.

Stoddard, Ellwyn R. *Maquila: Assembly Plants in Northern Mexico.* El Paso: Texas Western Press, 1987.

———. *Patterns of Poverty along the U.S.–Mexican Border.* El Paso: Center for Inter-American Studies, University of Texas at El Paso, 1978.

Tamayo, Jesús, and José Luis Fernández. *Zonas fronterizas (México–Estados Unidos).* México, D.F.: Centro de Investigación y Docencia Económicas, 1983.

Thorup, Cathryn L., ed. *The United States and Mexico: Face to Face with New Technology.* U.S. Third World Policy Perspectives no. 8. New Brunswick, N.J.: Transaction Books, 1987.

Torres Ramírez, Olga Ester. *La economía de frontera: El caso de la frontera norte de México.* México, D.F.: Aries, 1979.

U.S. General Accounting Office. *Health Care Availability in the Texas–Mexico Border Area: Report to the Honorable Lloyd Bentsen, U.S. Senate.* GAO/HRD-89-12. Washington, D.C.: GAO, 1988.

U.S. General Accounting Office. *Problems and Progress of Colonia Subdivisions near the Mexico Border: Report to the Chairman, Committee on Agriculture, House of Representatives.* GAO/RCED-91-37. Washington, D.C.: GAO, 1990.

Vanderwood, Paul J., and Frank N. Samponaro. *Border Fury: A Picture Postcard Record of Mexico's Revolution and U.S. War Preparedness, 1910–1917.* Albuquerque: University of New Mexico Press, 1988.

Weintraub, Sidney. *A Marriage of Convenience: Relations between Mexico and the United States.* New York: Oxford University Press, 1990.

————, ed. *U.S.–Mexico Industrial Integration: The Road to Free Trade.* Boulder, Colo.: Westview Press, 1991.

Weisman, Alan. *La Frontera: The United States Border with Mexico.* Photographs by Jay Desard. San Diego: Harcourt Brace Jovanovich, 1986.

A GUIDE TO LIBRARY RESEARCH ON BORDER-RELATED TOPICS

When preparing to research a border-related topic, keep in mind the variety of materials that may be consulted. These include books, articles in periodicals (newspapers, magazines, and scholarly journals), and government documents. Other possible library resources are maps, audiovisual material, archival material, and microforms (e.g., unpublished dissertations on microfilm). Also, some libraries or research centers keep vertical file material that can include brochures, pamphlets, newspaper clippings, photographs, and journal article reprints. The following is meant as a basic guide to these resources, but is by no means comprehensive.

Books

Books can be accessed through the library's card or computerized catalog. Most academic libraries use subject headings developed by the Library of Congress.

For general works, consult the following Library of Congress subject headings:
•Mexican American Border Region
•Mexico—Boundaries—United States
•Mexico—Foreign Relations—United States
•United States—Boundaries—Mexico
•United States—Foreign Relations—Mexico

For works on specific states, cities, or regions, look under their place names. Specific aspects of a subject will appear as subdivisions, or subheadings, e.g.:
•Ciudad Juárez—Economic conditions
•Rio Grande Valley—Commerce
•Sonora—History
•South Texas—Social conditions

Additional useful subheadings or subdivisions include:
•Addresses, essays, lectures
•Economic policy
•Emigration and immigration
•Industries
•Population
•Statistics

Other headings that may be useful are:
- Alien Labor, Mexican—United States
- Aliens, Illegal
- Chamizal (Mexican and Texas)
- Electronic Industries—Mexico
- International Boundary and Water Commission
- Labor and Laboring Classes—Mexico
- Mexican Americans
- Migrant Labor
- Offshore Assembly Industry
- Pollution—Mexico
- Southwest, New
- Tourist Trade—Mexico
- Water Resources Development
- Water Supply—Southwestern states
- Women Textile Workers
- Women—Employment—Mexico

Articles

Articles in journals, magazines, and newspapers can be located through the bibliographies and reference aids listed in Chapter 10 or through periodical indexes. In addition to printed indexes, there are other formats available including computerized data bases, CD-ROMs (Compact Disk–Read Only Memory), and computer-output microfilm. Among the nonprint indexing services on the market are *Newsearch, National Newspaper Index, Magazine Index,* and *InfoTrac.* Availability and cost of these services will vary from library to library.

Printed Periodical Indexes

Chicano Index. Boston: G. K. Hall, 1981, 1983; Berkeley: Chicano Studies Library Publications Unit, University of California, Berkeley, 1985–.

Articles appearing in Mexican American periodicals since 1967 are indexed comprehensively, while periodicals with primarily non-Latino content are selectively indexed. Subject, author, and title access are provided. As of 1989, this index—previously entitled the *Chicano Periodical Index*—has undergone a title and format change. It is now also available in CD-ROM format as the *Chicano Database.*

HAPI: Hispanic American Periodicals Index. Los Angeles: Latin American Center Publications, University of California, Los Angeles, 1975–.

This index provides subject and author access to "articles, documents, reviews, bibliographies, original literary works, and other items appearing in nearly 250 journals published throughout the world that regularly contain information on Latin America." It is now also available online.

PAIS Bulletin. New York: Public Affairs Information Service, Inc., 1915–.

In addition to articles in periodicals, this index includes books, government publications, pamphlets, and reports of private and quasi-governmental agencies.

Reader's Guide to Periodical Literature. New York: H. W. Wilson, 1900–.

Articles in popular magazines such as *Time, Newsweek,* and *Business Week* can be located using this very accessible index.

Social Sciences Index. New York: H. W. Wilson, 1974–.

This publication indexes scholarly social science journals, such as the *Journal of Interamerican Studies and World Affairs* and *Foreign Affairs.*

Printed Newspaper Indexes

Los Angeles Times Index. Ann Arbor, Mich.: University Microfilms International, 1972–.

New York Times Index. New York: New York Times Co., 1851–.

Official Washington Post Index. Woodbridge, Conn.: Research Publications, 1971–.

NewsBank Index. New Canaan, Conn.: NewsBank, Inc., 1970–.

This reference tool (available also in CD-ROM) indexes microfiche reproductions of articles published in over 450 U.S. dailies, including newspapers in border cities.

Clipping Services

ISLA: Information Services on Latin America. Berkeley, Calif.: ISLA, 1970–.

ISLA will duplicate and send to subscribers articles from major U.S. and European dailies. In addition to the newspapers that have indexes listed above, it includes the *Christian Science Monitor,* the *Miami Herald,* and the *Wall Street Journal.*

U.S. Government Documents

United States government documents are underutilized sources that very often contain information unavailable elsewhere.

Monthly Catalog of United States Government Publications. Washington, D.C.: Government Printing Office, 1895–.

The most comprehensive index to official publications of the U.S. government, the *Monthly Catalog* includes studies, reports, journals, pamphlets, and books issued by the various agencies and offices of the executive, legislative, and judicial branches of government. Providing author, subject, and title indexes, it is issued monthly, with semiannual cumulations.

Telephone Directories

Telephone directories are important sources of current information concerning border communities. We suggest consulting them for the hundreds of groups that, because of space limitations, we were unable to include in this guide. The listings under government agencies are especially useful. Telephone directories are available for most Mexican communities, and Mexican listings are also often included in the directories of their U.S. neighbors. On the U.S. side, telephone directories are available for the following cities or regions: Rio Grande Valley, Laredo, Eagle Pass, Del Rio, Las Cruces, Douglas, Nogales, Yuma, Imperial County, and San Diego. To purchase these directories call 1-800-792-2655.

APPENDIXES

A.1 REGIONS OF THE U.S.–MEXICO BORDER

States, Counties, Cities, Municipios, & Other Features	Border Crossings*

LOWER RIO GRANDE VALLEY–TAMAULIPAS BORDER REGION

TEXAS
Counties: Cameron, Hidalgo, Starr, & Zapata
Cities: Brownsville, San Benito, Harlingen, La Feria, Mercedes, Weslaco, Donna, Alamo, San Juan, Pharr, McAllen, Edinburg, Mission, Rio Grande City, & Roma
Other: Falcon Dam

TAMAULIPAS
Municipios: Matamoros, Valle Hermoso, Río Bravo, Reynosa, Gustavo Díaz Ordaz, Camargo, Miguel Alemán, & Ciudad Mier

Brownsville–Matamoros [2 bridges]

Progreso–Nuevo Progreso

Hidalgo–Reynosa

Los Ebanos–Gustavo Díaz Ordaz [ferry]

Rio Grande City–Camargo

Roma–Miguel Alemán

Falcon Dam [crossing]

LAREDO–NUEVO LAREDO (LOS DOS LAREDOS)

TEXAS
County: Webb
City: Laredo

TAMAULIPAS
Municipio: Nuevo Laredo

NUEVO LEÓN
Municipio: Colombia

Laredo–Nuevo Laredo [2 bridges]

Laredo–Colombia

*Unless noted otherwise, listings in this column indicate one bridge.

States, Counties, Cities, Municipios, & Other Features	Border Crossings*

EAGLE PASS–PIEDRAS NEGRAS—DEL RIO–ACUÑA REGION

TEXAS
Counties: Maverick, Kinney, & Val Verde
Cities: Eagle Pass & Del Rio
Other: Amistad Dam

COAHUILA
Municipios: Miguel Hidalgo, Guerrero,
Piedras Negras, & Ciudad Acuña

Eagle Pass–Piedras Negras

Del Rio–Ciudad Acuña

Amistad Dam [crossing]

BIG BEND—COAHUILAN & CHIHUAHUAN DESERTS REGION

TEXAS
Counties: Terrell, Brewster, Presidio,
Jeff Davis, & Hudspeth
City (unincorporated): Presidio
Other: Big Bend National Park

COAHUILA
Municipio: Ocampo (which includes
the village of Boquillas)

CHIHUAHUA
Municipios: Manuel Benavides &
Ojinaga

La Linda mine (northeast of
Big Bend)

Presidio–Ojinaga

EL PASO—CIUDAD JUÁREZ AREA

TEXAS
County: El Paso
City: El Paso

CHIHUAHUA
Municipios: Guadalupe Bravos, Praxedis
G. Guerrero, & Ciudad Juárez

El Paso–Juárez metro. area
[6 bridges]

States, Counties, Cities, Municipios, & Other Features	Border Crossings*

NEW MEXICO–CHIHUAHUA BORDERLANDS

NEW MEXICO
Counties: Doña Ana, Luna, & Hidalgo

City: Las Cruces
Village: Columbus

CHIHUAHUA
Municipios: Ciudad Juárez & Ascensión
(which includes the community of Gen.
Rodrigo Quevedo)

Columbus–Gen. Rodrigo
Quevedo

Antelope Wells (N. Mex.)

ARIZONA–SONORA BORDERLANDS

ARIZONA
Counties: Cochise, Santa Cruz, Pima, &
Yuma
Cities: Douglas, Bisbee, Naco, Nogales,
& Yuma
Other: Organ Pipe National Monument

SONORA
Municipios: Agua Prieta, Naco, Cananea,
Santa Cruz, Nogales, Saric, Altar, Ca-
borca, Puerto Peñasco, & San Luis Río
Colorado

Douglas–Agua Prieta

Naco–Naco

Nogales–Nogales

Sasabe–Sasabe

Lukeville–Sonoita

San Luis–San Luis Río Colorado

CALIFORNIA–BAJA CALIFORNIA BORDER REGION

CALIFORNIA
Counties: Imperial & San Diego
Cities: Calexico, San Ysidro, Chula Vista,
& San Diego

BAJA CALIFORNIA
Municipios: Mexicali, Tecate, & Tijuana

Andrade–Algodones

Calexico–Mexicali

Tecate–Tecate

San Diego–Tijuana

183

A.2 POPULATIONS OF MAJOR U.S.–MEXICO BORDER CROSSING POINTS, 1950 TO MID-1980s

	1950	1960	1970	1980	mid-1980s (estimated)
ARIZONA*					
Douglas	9,442	11,925	12,462	13,058	14,135
Agua Prieta	13,121	17,248	23,272	34,380	48,412
Nogales	6,155	7,286	8,946	15,683	19,275
Nogales	24,480	39,812	53,494	68,076	84,096
Yuma	9,145	23,974	29,007	43,057	50,000
San Luis Río Colorado	13,593	42,134	63,604	92,790	129,211
CALIFORNIA*					
Calexico	6,433	7,992	10,625	14,412	15,850
Mexicali	64,658	281,333	396,324	510,664	738,345
San Diego	334,387	573,224	697,471	875,538	1,000,000
Tijuana	59,950	165,690	340,583	461,257	856,742
TEXAS*					
Brownsville	36,066	48,040	52,522	84,997	100,000
Matamoros	45,737	143,043	186,146	238,840	297,177
Del Rio	14,211	18,612	21,330	30,034	35,000
Ciudad Acuña	—	—	32,500	41,948	52,466
Eagle Pass	7,267	12,094	15,364	21,407	25,000
Piedras Negras	27,578	48,408	46,698	80,290	101,020
El Paso	130,485	276,687	322,261	425,259	516,996
Ciudad Juárez	122,566	276,995	424,135	567,365	923,713
Laredo	51,510	60,678	69,024	91,449	106,330
Nuevo Laredo	57,669	96,043	151,253	203,286	288,057
McAllen	20,067	32,728	37,636	67,042	75,000
Reynosa	34,076	134,869	150,768	211,412	284,318

*Cities are listed by U.S. state, with Mexican cities in italics.

SOURCES

The population figures for 1950–80 were drawn from *Censos Generales de Población* (México, D.F.: Dirección General de Estadísticas, 1950–80) and *Census of Population* (Washington, D.C.: U.S. Bureau of the Census, 1950–80).

Although much higher population figures are often given for Mexican border communities for 1980, we chose to use the more conservative figures available from the official census, since, as James Peach points out, "the intent of the government of Mexico was to provide a complete and accurate count of the number of persons residing in Mexico," and the census data are consistent both internally and with the results of earlier surveys. "Thus, until there is quantitative evidence to the contrary, there is no alternative but to regard the results of the 1980 Census of Population and Housing in Mexico as the most comprehensive and accurate available" (James T. Peach, "Demographic and Economic Change in Mexico's Northern Frontier: Evidence from the *X Censo General de Población y Vivienda*," Latin American Research Paper Series, no. 2 [Las Cruces, N.Mex.: New Mexico State University, 1984], 6).

The last column gives population estimates for the middle to late 1980s. These were drawn from a variety of sources. Estimates for all Mexican cities are for 1989 and were provided by the Departamento de Estudios de Población of the Colegio de la Frontera Norte. Brownsville, McAllen, Eagle Pass, Del Rio, and San Diego figures are for 1986 and were drawn from the *Statistical Abstract of the United States*, 108th ed. (Washington, D.C.: U.S. Department of Commerce, Bureau of the Census, 1988). (It should be noted that San Diego County has a population of over 2,000,000.) The figure for El Paso is for 1988 and was furnished by the Research and Planning Division of the Department of Planning of the City of El Paso. Arizona border community population estimates were provided by the Arizona Department of Commerce. Nogales and Yuma figures are for 1987, and the Douglas figure is for 1988.

In the case of Tijuana, many local planners use a population figure of at least 1,000,000. One study from Baja California lists the 1980 Tijuana population as 659,500, the 1985 estimate as 858,207, the 1990 projection as 1,129,000, and the year 2000 projection as 1,815,000 ("Plan de Desarrollo Urbano, Centro de Población, Ciudad de Tijuana," cited in *The Bridge* [San Diego Association of Governments, 1988], 27).

A.3 NUMBER OF PEOPLE ENTERING THE UNITED STATES AT MEXICO BORDER CROSSINGS, FISCAL YEAR 1986

ARIZONA	22,620,948
Douglas	4,938,753
Lukeville	539,891
Naco	919,580
Nogales	10,591,790
San Luis	5,590,924
Sasabe	40,010
CALIFORNIA	61,329,617
Andrade	836,212
Calexico	15,957,885
San Ysidro	34,142,918
Tecate	3,991,864
Otay Mesa	6,400,738
NEW MEXICO	938,114
Columbus	938,114
TEXAS	101,757,381
Amistad Dam	87,190
Brownsville	14,179,733
Del Rio	3,113,663
Eagle Pass	5,450,207
El Paso	32,842,994
Fabens	1,014,245
Falcon Heights	259,882
Fort Hancock	*not listed*
Hidalgo	13,440,088
Juárez–Lincoln Bridge	8,928,471
Laredo	11,752,405
Los Ebanos	205,333
Presidio	888,857
Progreso	3,647,177
Rio Grande City	1,556,846
Roma	4,390,290
Total Crossings	186,646,060

Source: Immigration and Naturalization Service, United States Department of Justice.

A.4   PUBLIC HEALTH ORGANIZATIONS ON THE BORDER

Southwest Border Rural Health Research Center

One of five Rural Health Research Centers in the United States, this center serves as an information resource for the states of California, Arizona, New Mexico, and Texas. Its primary research interests are patterns of health-care utilization by Mexican nationals in the United States, and medical liability issues affecting the availability of health care in rural areas of the four U.S. border states.

Southwest Border Rural Health Research Center
3131 East Second
Tucson, Arizona 85721
(602) 626-7946
Director: Andrew Nichols, M.D.

United States–Mexico Border Health Association / Asociación Fronteriza Mexicana–Estadounidense de Salud

Established in the early 1940s, this organization has over 1,000 members. It receives support from the Pan American Health Organization of the World Health Organization and from the U.S. and Mexican governments, as well as from membership dues. The original purpose of the association was to encourage cooperation among health agencies and workers in both countries; it remains the major organization promoting the exchange of health information between the United States and Mexico. The association publishes a newsletter at least three times a year, and has published a quarterly journal, *Border Health/Salud Fronteriza,* since 1985. It holds an annual meeting each spring. Regional and local branch organizations also hold meetings in different cities along the border.

U.S.–Mexico Border Health Association
6006 North Mesa Street, suite 600
El Paso, Texas 79912
(915) 581-6645

A.5 CHAMBERS OF COMMERCE, U.S. BORDER CITIES

In addition to providing current information about cross-border activities of local community groups, chambers of commerce can supply basic information regarding demographic and economic trends in their area.

Arizona

Ajo Chamber of Commerce
P.O. Box 507
Ajo, Arizona 85321
(602) 387-7059

Bisbee Chamber of Commerce
Drawer BA
Bisbee, Arizona 85603
(602) 432-2141

Douglas Chamber of Commerce
Drawer F
Douglas, Arizona 85607
(602) 364-2477

Nogales Chamber of Commerce
Kino Park
Nogales, Arizona 85621
(602) 287-3685

Sierra Vista Chamber of Commerce
372 North Garden Avenue
Sierra Vista, Arizona 85635
(602) 458-6940

Yuma Chamber of Commerce
377 South Main Street
P.O. Box 230
Yuma, Arizona 85366
(602) 782-2567

California

Calexico Chamber of Commerce
1100 West Imperial
Calexico, California 92231
(714) 357-1166

Otay Mesa Chamber of Commerce
6698 Siempre Viva Road
San Ysidro, California 92073
(619) 661-6111

San Diego Chamber of Commerce
110 C Street, suite 1600
San Diego, California 92101
(619) 232-0124

San Ysidro Chamber of Commerce
268 West Park Avenue
San Ysidro, California 92073
(619) 428-1281

New Mexico

Las Cruces Chamber of Commerce
760 West Picacho
P.O. Box 519
Las Cruces, New Mexico 88004
(505) 524-1968

Texas

Brownsville Chamber of Commerce
P.O. Drawer 752
Brownsville, Texas 78520
(512) 542-4341

Del Rio Chamber of Commerce
P.O. Box 1388
Del Rio, Texas 78840
(512) 775-3551

Eagle Pass Chamber of Commerce
P.O. Box 1188
Eagle Pass, Texas 78852
(512) 773-3224

El Paso Chamber of Commerce
10 Civic Center Plaza
El Paso, Texas 79901
(915) 544-7880

Laredo Chamber of Commerce
P.O. Box 1511
Laredo, Texas 78040
(512) 722-9895

McAllen Chamber of Commerce
10 North Broadway
McAllen, Texas 78501
(512) 682-2871

Rio Grande Valley Chamber of
  Commerce
P.O. Box 975
Weslaco, Texas 78596
(512) 968-3141

A.6 PRIVATE BORDER ORGANIZATIONS

BILATERAL COMMISSION ON THE FUTURE OF UNITED STATES–MEXICAN RELATIONS

Although the commission received informal approval and encouragement from both the U.S. and Mexican governments, it was made up of private citizens who came together to promote mutually advantageous long-term relations between the two countries. Formed in 1986, and now inactive, the commission was co-chaired by Hugo Margáin, former Mexican ambassador to the United States, and former U.S. Department of State undersecretary William D. Rogers. A report that included a section on the border was published in 1988 (*see Chapter 10, section 3, for full reference*).

INTERNATIONAL GOOD NEIGHBOR COUNCIL / CONSEJO INTERNACIONAL DE BUENA VECINDAD

This council, founded in 1954 in Monterrey, Nuevo León, is an association of some 2,000 business and professional people interested in maintaining good relations between the United States and Mexico. It was created under the auspices of the Texas Good Neighbor Commission. The United States and Mexican sections of the organization work together and hold two conventions each year, one in Texas and one in Mexico. In addition to the main offices in Monterrey, there are regional offices in northern Mexico and Texas.

International Good Neighbor Council
P.O. Box 1689
McAllen, Texas 78501
President: Arnaldo Ramírez

Consejo Internacional de Buena Vecindad
Edificio Latino
Juan Ignacio Ramón 506 Oriente, despacho 513
64000 Monterrey, Nuevo León
Tel. 42-7633
Executive Director: Jorge García de Alba C.

MEXICO–TEXAS BRIDGE OWNERS ASSOCIATION

Most decisions regarding the site locations, construction, and mainte-
nance of bridges and crossings along the border are the responsibilities of
the U.S. and Mexican federal governments. Nevertheless, the Mexico–
Texas Bridge Owners Association has played an important role in this
decision-making process. It represents the interest of Texas bridge owners, and has been a major informal actor in negotiations with the Mexican government concerning the selection of bridge sites.

Mexico–Texas Bridge Owners Association
P.O. Drawer H
Rio Grande City, Texas 78582
(512) 487 3396

A.7 TELEPHONE AREA CODES FOR MEXICO

The listings for Mexico in this guide do not include the area codes. To reach a number in Mexico, first dial 011, then 52 (the country code for Mexico), and the area code for the city desired. For example, to call the U.S. Consulate in Tijuana (Tel. 81-7400) from the United States, dial 011–52–66–81-7400. The area codes for Mexican border communities and other cities listed in the directory are provided here.

BAJA CALIFORNIA

Mexicali: 65
Tecate: 665
Tijuana: 66

CHIHUAHUA

Ciudad Juárez: 16
General Rodrigo Quevedo: 166
Ojinaga: 145

COAHUILA

Ciudad Acuña: 877
Piedras Negras: 878
Saltillo: 841

DISTRITO FEDERAL (D.F.)

Mexico City: 5

NUEVO LEÓN

Monterrey: 83

SONORA

Agua Prieta: 633
Hermosillo: 621
Naco: 633
Nogales: 631
San Luis Río Colorado: 653
Sonoita: 651

TAMAULIPAS

Camargo: 827
Gustavo Díaz Ordaz: 892
Matamoros: 891
Nuevo Laredo: 871
Reynosa: 892
Río Bravo: 893
Valle Hermosa: 894

About the Authors

MILTON H. JAMAIL holds an M.A. from the University of Houston and a Ph.D. from the University of Arizona. In 1982, he received a Senior Fulbright Award to study water-resource issues in the U.S.–Mexico borderlands. He is currently lecturer in the government department of the University of Texas at Austin.

MARGO GUTIÉRREZ holds an M.L.S. from the University of Arizona and an M.A. from the Institute of Latin American Studies, University of Texas at Austin. She is the Mexican American studies librarian at the Benson Latin American Collection of the University of Texas at Austin.